RESEARCH ART

Michael Betancourt is a critical theorist and research artist who has cultivated a hybrid practice addressing media history, digital technology, and capitalist ideology. Author of more than thirty books, his deeply interdisciplinary writing has been translated into Chinese, French, German, Greek, Italian, Japanese, Persian, Portuguese, and Spanish. His critical analysis provides a model and foundation for his studio work. This analysis considers the contemporary global financialization of digital capitalism via the social and cultural impacts of AI, Bitcoin, surveillance, and Universal Basic Income (inter alia) as reflections of structural demands implicit in how the Enlightenment project informs both historical industrial capitalism and contemporary digital technology. He is a board member of the *Art of Light Organization.*

As a pioneer of "Glitch Art," he has engaged the links between theory and practice by databending images and video since the 1990s. His visually seductive glitch works bring the visionary tradition into the present. By emphasizing their digital origins, his aesthetics encourages the viewer to find poetic meaning in their everyday life. His movies and statics have shown internationally at film festivals and art fairs, including the *Black Maria Film Festival, Art Basel Miami Beach, Contemporary Art Ruhr, Athens Video Art Festival, Festival des Cinemas Differents de Paris, Anthology Film Archives, Millennium Film Workshop,* the San Francisco Cinematheque's *Crossroads,* and *Experiments in Cinema,* among others. One of his games-as-art, *Toonzy! The Cartoon Role-Playing Game,* was nominated for an Ennie Award as *Best Free Game* in 2016. His interactive publication the ____________ *Manifesto* is a well known work of interactive net.art from the 1990s. This aesthetic work is informed by ground breaking historical research: in 2006, he found the oldest surviving hand-painted abstract films (produced in 1916 by Mary Hallock-Greenewalt). He also wrote the first history of motion graphics in the United States charting its origins to the commercial appropriation of avant-garde film and video art.

His archive is located at *michaelbetancourt.com*

RESEARCH ART

glitches, poetics, typography and the aura of the digital

Michael Betancourt

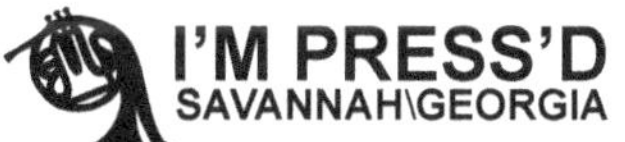

Published by I'M PRESS'D
Distributed by Cinegraphic Media
Typeset in Times New Roman

for Leah

www.michaelbetancourt.com

Instaglitches originally posted online in the *@glitcharts* account on *Instagram*; and in the *Instaglitches: 2018—2020* portfolio (2021, 931 pp.) https://archive.org/details/instaglitches-2018-2020

A version of Chapter 1 was originally published on *Cinegraphic.net* (July 24, 2021).

A version of Chapter 2 was originally published in *Utsanga.it,* #15.

Parts of Chapter 3 were adapted from *Cinematic Articulation in Motion Graphics* published by Routledge, 2022.

Figure 4.1 originally published in *Leonardo* vol. 48, no. 5 (2015).

Figure 4.2 originally published in *Canyon Cinemazine #6* (2019).

A version of Chapter 5 was originally published in *The Decadent Review.*

A version of Chapter 6 was originally published in *Utsanga.it,* #28.

ISBN 978-0-9793215-0-4

CONTENTS

This book is a manifesto that documents artistic research independent of the aesthetic concerns of the studio; it is neither a description of praxis nor an extra-artistic justification for art, but is instead a series of secondary responses to the process and discoveries made while and by making art. The discussion that follows presents an artist's critical thinking about their own work in a larger context of conceptual and theoretical concerns that are neither a statement of intentions, nor merely a subjective series of claims about their artistic accomplishments.

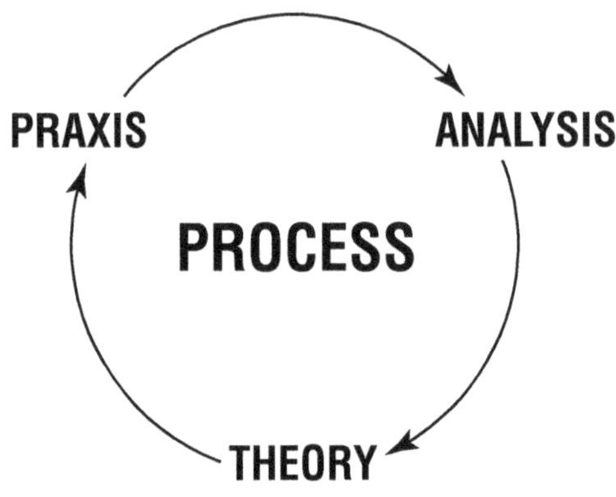

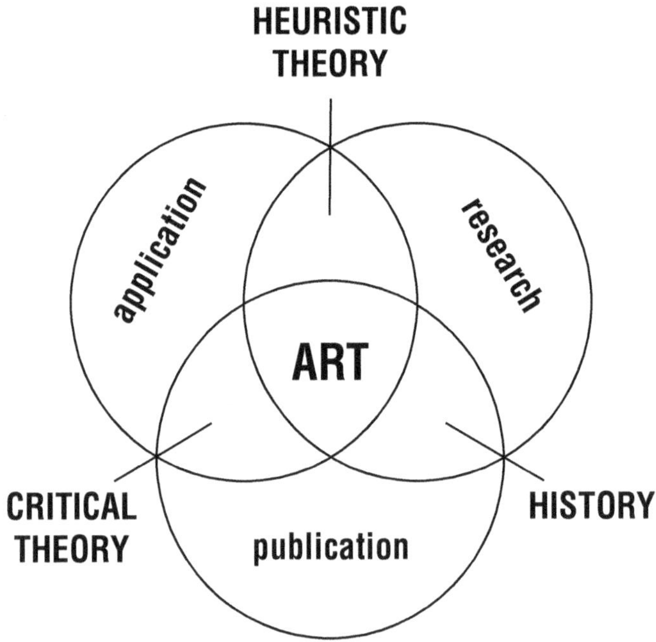

Figure 1.1: [top] The connections between theory, praxis and analysis; [bottom] the varieties of work this approach produces in my studio practice.

1

DEFINING "*RESEARCH ART*"

Composer John Cage noted the 'problem of history' in the 1950s; it is an issue that has grown more important, rather than less, in the decades since. Artists adopting a self-conscious positioning in relation to a specific history (tradition)—whether in a sense of continuing it, or in the sense of escaping from it—unifies the positivistic dimensions of Modernism and Post-Modernist alike. To the extent that the Contemporary embrace of relativism is "ahistorical," it is not an escape from this avant-guardiste positivism, but a response to the post-structural critique that introduced a plurality of directions that now dominate discourse within the gallery-fair-museum network. This expansion of aesthetic opportunity has not minimized the need for self-conscious positioning, it has starkly highlighted it. The issue in confronting the Contemporary is to separate emotional, dialectical, traditional conceptions of "opposition" and "resistance" (the heritage of the avant-garde) to consider a tactical relaction that demonstrates Cage's koan-like observation:

> One does not then just any experiment, but does what must be done; one does not seek by his actions to arrive at money, but does what must be done; one does not seek by his actions to arrive at fame (success), but one does what must be done; but does what must be done; one does not seek by his actions to provide pleasure to the senses (beauty), but one does what must be done; one doe not seek by his actions to arrive at the establishment of a school (truth), but one does what must be done. One does something else. What else?[1]

The 'new move' is *the* problem: it is a contingency defined by the immanent and immediate situation confronting the artist working. 'New' is not a given, but a relational construct—new on what terms? Addressing this question changes over time because it is a discursive problem, (a descriptive apparatus that establishes the limina enabling Contemporary actions), and in the process identifies potentially unrecognizable potentials: what the "correct" action is emerges as a feature of analysis—it can only be determined in relation to the 'pieces in play'—from the 'aesthetic field' being addressed, as Arthur Danto has observed about the development of art addressing its assumed boundaries in the 1950s and 1960s:

> The philosophical question of the nature of art, rather, was something that arose within art [following the 1960s] when artists pressed against boundary after boundary, and found that all the boundaries gave way.[2]

Danto's analysis assumes a fixed, stable definition for "art," one that no longer applies in the Contemporary. However, his concern with limina, margins, and boundaries is another way of identifying challenges to what the dominant conceptions of "art" were. His analysis describes a foundational shift from the unitary and fixed conception of the "aesthetic" (which was subject to debate during Modernism) to an expansion whose initial recognition derives from rupture of those limitations typical of the historical avant-gardes (the Post-Modern). Clement Greenberg's attempt at constructing an opposition between Modernism and the avant-garde[3] was doomed from the start precisely due to his picking sides in this debate: thus his rejection in the Post-Modern arises from his having picked the losing side in what is now clearly a disagreement over approach. The Contemporary which emerges in the aftermath of this debate is at the same time the success of the avant-garde's attack on established institutional power and authority over who provides the definition of "art"—which is the substance of Danto's argument. As Paul Virilio asked about the historical avant-gardes, "in advance of what?"—the answer arrives with the Contemporary gallery-fair-museum network and its opening of aesthetic boundaries to an 'expanded field' of potentials.[4] The unqualified dominance of the avant-garde's expansive definition also matches the demands for an expansive valorization in globalized capitalism by embracing all those works that might be considered "aesthetic" whatever their form, basis, or status historically; this account of aesthetic development begins during the 1970s and 1980s, but also corresponds to the dominance of post-structuralism—what has come *after* is neither an "end to art" nor a degeneration into an "anything goes." This aesthetic domain shapes the *paysage* that determines heuristics—the choices (mobilization) of which constitute the actions taken within that metaphoric space. Cage's comments return within this domain (which they helped propose) as an understanding that posits 'historical processes' as *un*directional: neither positivist nor relativist, 'aesthetics' become contingent positions adopted within a shifting field of allowances and refusals (as on the *Go* board) whose importance shifts over time, yet unlike that game which gradually fills and holds the all available positions, once filled spaces are continually being cleared away as the "game" progresses. The superficially "retrograde" and repetitive nature of the Contemporary reflects this process of valorization/renovation that masks itself as both 'critical' and 'innovation' or 'new.'

"Emptying the board" is a metaphor that clarifies the linkage between aesthetic practice and capitalist economics that has become prominent in the Contemporary. It suggests an 'aesthetic cycle' comparable to the 'business cycle'—where nothing remains over time and the earlier avant-gardes become revitalized as genres for valorization by the gallery-fair-museum network.[5] Understanding this process depends on the recognition that when linked to aesthetics, *capitalism is not a system of production, but a method of articulating social position.* The traditional definition of capitalism as 'an economic system where human labor becomes a commodity traded in itself' obscures the *use value* of aesthetics and artistic production: demonstrating the hierarchal organization of human society—*capitalism as a management of commodity access and distribution*. The price of art is not a reflection of importance, but a sorting mechanism that imposes class distinctions where the most rarified, expensive objects are tokens signifying social position in addition to (or in spite of) whatever their aesthetics and critical meanings may be. Oppositions between the parts of society that are directed (and thus beholden to perform actions for higher ranking members of society) and those parts of society that direct others is not a simple binary opposition, but a scale of increasing authority and control even within these superficially distinct groupings; aesthetics—embraced, rejected—help define membership and position by serving as stand-ins for this hierarchy.

These anthropological understandings of art and the art world identify an authoritarian dimension that is both essential and invisible to the social organization of capitalism, whether centralized, as in the command economies of the "communist" countries such as the Soviet Union and People's Republic of China, or dispersed in the "market" economies of the United States and Europe. They are twin poles within the same *capitalist* range. Business even identifies this productive space with the avant-gardist proposition of "Creative Destruction" where the mechanism of clearing-away is technological change that results in the continuous demand for 'innovation,' as economist Joseph Schumpeter explained in the 1950s:

> The opening up of new markets, foreign or domestic, and the organizational development from the craft shop and factory to such concerns as U.S. Steel illustrate the same process of industrial mutation—if I may use that biological term—that incessantly revolutionizes the economic structure *from within,* incessantly destroying the old one, incessantly creating a new one. This process of Creative Destruction is the essential fact about capitalism.[6]

Money makes the capitalist "world go 'round" precisely because money is the mechanism determining social position within both the centralized and market varieties of capitalism; the difference between this development following industrialization and that of the pre-industrial world lies with how the limitations on commodity access becomes less a function of limited availability than an increasingly pure expression of social status expressed via the gallery-fair-museum network that defines the Contemporary art world. The production/valorization processes of industrial capitalism are distinct from those of aesthetic production, yet their relationships and connections are clearly articulated by recognizing the isomorphic parity of "Creative Destruction" and the historical avant-garde's nihilism and alienation that sought to liquidate the art world in favor of radically shifting definitions for what constituted "art." The dominance of this ideation plays out during the twentieth century first as Modernism, then more specifically in the dominance of the avant-garde.

Prior to industrialization, organizing production was the central problem for society since all production was limited by scarcity and the difficulty of manufacturing; the resulting tendency to overproduction made possible by industrialization created periodic panics in the mismatch of production/consumption that resulted in bankrupt businesses. This cycle was driven in part by translations of disinterested (non-market-based) research into commercial applications. The instability that Schumpeter terms "Creative Destruction" derives from this process and mirrors artist Andy Warhol's conception of "Business Art":

> Business art is the step that comes after art. I started as a commercial artist, and I want to finish as a business artist. Being good in business is the most fascinating kind of art. During the hippie era people put down the idea of business. They'd say "money is bad" and "working is bad." But making money is art, and working is art—and good business is the best art.[7]

This repudiation of Romantic conceptions of artistic activity and production embraces capitalism, recapitulating Warhol's' other mirrorings of capitalist production throughout his praxis: the factory (his studio itself), silk-screen reproduction, and assembly-line labor employed in the production of his work. His translation of these capitalist economic relations makes the subordination of aesthetic actions by the artist to their market explicit as the "price" paid for entrance to the art world: artistic productions that circulate within the gallery-fair-museum network are economic productions. However, a different problem confronts industrial society, one that became apparent in the first industrial revolution as scarcity of resources and labor became secondary to the question of how to distribute production: who is allowed access to what amount, type, and quality of commodity. Increases in productivity, efficiency, and quantity/quality establish the distribution problem as a distinct issue apart from production itself. Economics transforms the basis of this question about accessing production into the reification of caste and class hidden by questions of costs and allocation of wealth. The superficially "fluid" dynamics of social mobility and position in this capitalist system of distribution are suppressed via the fixed structures of accumulated wealth and inherited position. This mechanism for organizing society—the amount of money controlled by an individual—was historically an expression of rights to distribute the products of labor already performed. The nature of that receipt for past production, whether gold, silver, paper, or anything else did not matter so long as it was socially accepted and its value unquestioned.

Digital capitalism neither replaces nor challenges the existing structures of capitalist social organization; instead, it attempts to render them resilient to (technological, social) challenge by transforming the dynamics and complexity of human action into a predetermined (and thus controlled) set of contingent privileges subject to revoke: the transfer of social position into the reifications of digital systems and their autonomous policing of rights to access and activity. The renovation of aesthetics within this 'expanded field' corresponds to the expansive aspects of capitalism, which as critics such as Terry Smith[8] and C. B. Johnson have noted,[9] now corresponds to the entirety of the "art world" that matches the transnational, borderless economic flows and circulations of globalization. Economic power is now synonymous with cultural authority, as Smith observes:

> Contemporary art, as a movement, has become the new Modern, or, what amounts to the same thing, the old Modern in new clothes. In its most institutionalized forms [...] it is the latest phase in the

> century-and-a-half-long story of Modern art in Europe and its cultural colonies, a continuation of the Modernist lineage, warily selected not least in at attempt to preserve this cultural balance of power.[10]

Contemporary cultural authority expands the reach of the twentieth century globally. Art and its affective role as a social practice, is readily identified with being a material commodity; this discarding of Romanticism's transcendent pretexts is Warhol's "Business Art" as the entirety of artistic practice.[11] These shifts were underway during the 1960s, apparent in movements such as Pop Art and Conceptual Art, that developed in parallel to the invention of digital computers.[12] Their convergence with networking technology becomes obvious during the 1990s as digital capitalism emerged into dominance.[13] The 'question' that "Business Art" poses is readily apparent from its complicity with capitalist concerns: in being fully assimilated to the marketplace, this apparatus of cultural and social forces compromises any proposition of an independent, critical media within the 'art world' by its necessary connections to marketing and popularity that constrain and elide the 'degrees of freedom' afforded to posing any challenges. The assumption that the marketplace will embrace and assimilate any counter-production is an obvious tautology since works not assimilated are also "invisible" to its propositional/critical apparatus.

Aesthetics that valorize these relationships are familiar. They remain within an historically-assigned critical appearance, yet are at the same time unquestionably complicit with social demands for exclusivity and allure specific to art-products. The transformation of conceptual "happenings" into exclusionary events for wealthy patrons in Relational Art during the 1990s demonstrates the interlocking economic and aesthetic practices of the Contemporary. Nicolas Bourriaud, the curator closely associated with defining this shift explains its practical implementation:

> [1990's] art thus prompts us to envisage the relations between space and time in a different way. Essentially,

> moreover, it derives its main originality from the way this issue is handled. What, actually, is *concretely produced* by artists such as Liam Gillick, Dominique Gonzales-Foerster and Vanessa Beecroft? What, in the final analysis, is the object of their work?[14]

The creation of art/event-spectacles that leave no 'art object' afterwards in the way that even Conceptual Art left behind *things* that can be collected, exhibited, and examined as aesthetic production does not challenge the socially exclusive dimensions of globalized art-production, but makes them apparent. When there are no 'objects' to collect what is being produced is a 'bespoke social entertainment' for those patrons wealthy enough to afford it. The nature of the work is thus less significant for this consideration than its audience since the cultural dimensions of "Business Art" as social positioning are literal. The proposition of this work as 'critical' is dubious—although there are no "objects" to collect—it emphasizes replacing aesthetics with social relationships (the same foundation as currency) that invite its critique as an especially nepotistic and elitist variety of art. The proposition of such work as a critical challenge is untenable: capitalism itself enables the 'critical' structural enframing of Relational Art. The abstracted social value this work reifies is inversely correlated with the commercial value attached to that activity. This mismatch reifies 'Baumol's cost disease' in the arts: greater productivity does not result in changed costs or values produced. The affective shift to performance described by Nicholas Bourriaud's "relational aesthetics" valorizes those economic relationships capitalism identifies as foundational, in the process masking underlying *causa* that render this superstructure simply a symptom of an underlying order. Economic relations act as a proxy for class and social hierarchy, but are a response to a system of cultural value that differentiates between *inventive* and *implementive* roles for agency where the innovations of 'artistic labor' signifies cultural significance.

Identifying any alternative to these relationships, as posited by Cage's comments in *Silence*, requires rejections of the typical

Propositions for a "Research Art"

[**1**] Research art is conceptual (not formal) intervention.

[**2**] Research art engages with limina and other 'boundaries' (aesthetic, cultural, political, social).

[**3**] Research artists produce works challenging, exploring, problematizing, and revealing 'boundaries.'

[**4**] Research artists use the conventions of art to consider non-art conditions.

[**5**] Non-art contexts (aesthetic, cultural, political, social) are the material subjects of research art.

[**6**] Research art does not define the aesthetic rules of the past more precisely, but rather investigates new rules.

[**7**] Research art is a cultural practice.

[**8**] The "research" in "research art" concerns the empirical cues in the art work that direct the audiences' interpretive engagement.

[**9**] Meaning is an imposition, mediated by past experience, subjective desire, and empirical recognitions.

[**10**] Any media are appropriate provided they correspond to the parameters required by the research.

cultural aesthetics/operations. In the case of the "Business Art" that dominates the contemporary, a refusal of the types Cage enumerates risks a slippage into the Romantic conceit of "art for art" that Warhol's proposal critiqued (before becoming dominant). Approaching this dispositive necessarily appears "academic," a diagnosis, seeking to define the parameters of the "field" to allow a consideration of its potentials and *which* "moves" remain primarily independent of its economic demands.

Cultural capital, like cultural authority, is a limited resource whose allotment and extension is controlled directly by gate keepers and indirectly by gate keeping organizations: *whose works are valued, whose neglected?* The irony of privilege is not lost at the margins, even if it is tinted by obvious hypocrisy. To make any type of art begins from a place of privilege, wealth, and stability—however difficult creation may actually be. The revelation that what historically was *not* of interest to contending elites has now become a reflection of the same class distinctions that inform the art world as a whole should not come as a shock: to see the social and class preoccupations of the art world refracting through the realm of the gallery-fair-museum network is a perfectly natural reflection of its members' identities.

However, from this concentration of cultural authority and its attendant exclusivity comes the familiar region: the marginalized. In the case of media it is a marginalization not primarily determined by content or form, but by technology. In other words, it is not an issue of aesthetics. For example, the rejection of movies for being "too digital" is a refusal of them for not announcing their photochemical-costliness as a criterion of significance. It is a perverse refusal since the rejection is precisely the Modernist demand for medium-specificity, but wielded as a weapon in a rejection of all works made with the "wrong" medium. Rather than being a historical curiosity, these concerns remain powerfully active even after the "end" of Modernism postulated

---

Figure 1.2: Publication replaces exhibition in "A Taxonomy of Abstract Form Using Studies of Synaesthesia and Hallucinations" by Michael Betancourt

THEORETICAL PERSPECTIVE

A Taxonomy of Abstract Form Using Studies of Synesthesia and Hallucinations

Michael Betancourt

ABSTRACT

The author proposes a taxonomy of abstract form anchored in an examination of the history and theory of synesthesia and abstract art. The foundations of this taxonomy lie in empirical psychological studies of "form-constants" found in cross-modal synesthetic visions and hallucinatory states, specifically the work of Heinrich Klüver in his examinations of mescaline and the mechanisms producing visual hallucinations. While the proposed taxonomy is limited only to synesthesia-inspired abstraction, it has suggestive possibilities when considered in relation to other forms of non-synesthetic abstraction such as Islamic Art, the geometric forms found on classical Greek vases, and other kinds of decorative abstract patterns.

Film historians William Moritz and William Wees have observed an overlap between the forms of hallucination/synesthesia and abstract film. The parallel histories of synesthesia, abstract painting and abstract film noted by these historians theoretically allows a consideration of synesthetic visual forms identified by psychology as the basis for a taxonomy of abstraction. This paper proposes a taxonomy of abstract form anchored in an examination of the history of synesthesia and abstract art. Existing work on abstract film, especially Wees's *Light Moving in Time*, suggests the possible utility of a taxonomy but does not provide one [1].

Because the taxonomy proposed here originates in Heinrich Klüver's study of mescaline hallucinations and Kevin Dann's discussion of synesthesia, a brief historical survey of the relationship between synesthesia and abstraction is appropriate. While any aesthetic taxonomy is necessarily a reification, a brief consideration of the historical context that justifies a taxonomy may suggest a degree of validity for some forms of abstraction.

DEFINITIONS

Because this paper employs a variety of terms drawn from art history and the study of synesthesia, a clear explanation of the terms is needed. The crucial, and most difficult to define, term in this taxonomy is "synesthesia." The use of "synesthesia" to describe art entails an ambiguity: Where for psychology "synesthesia" refers specifically to cross-modal sensory experiences, such as seeing colors at the same time as one hears sounds, in art its use is often metaphoric, identifying works that attempt to present analogues for one sense (such as hearing), typically sound or music, within another, most commonly visual, art such as painting. Bulat Galeyev has discussed these ambiguities in his "Open Letter on Synesthesia," noting that they are a part of the history of its use in art [2]. This ambiguity of use in discussion of art appears because "synesthesia" often refers to both the actual experience of synesthesia and its use as analogy in describing an artwork.

Within this framework, the term "hallucination" is needed to refer to subjectively encountered phenomena that individuals may experience. While "synesthesia" has an ambiguous meaning, "hallucination" retains its technical, clinical denotation.

As used in this paper, "abstract" refers to the broad understanding of the word identified by art historian Jeffrey Schnapp, which was employed at the beginning of the 20th century [3]. This conception "rarely meant *abstract* in any pure, rigorously formal, non-referential, non-representational visual sense" [4]; it was instead "hybrid" [5], a formulation that encompasses the overlap of abstraction in film and painting.

For historians such as William Moritz, those abstract filmmakers whose work focused on geometric forms, often synchronized to music, constitute an ongoing tradition of "visual music":

> Indeed, visual music has a history that parallels that of cinema itself. For centuries artists and philosophers theorized that there

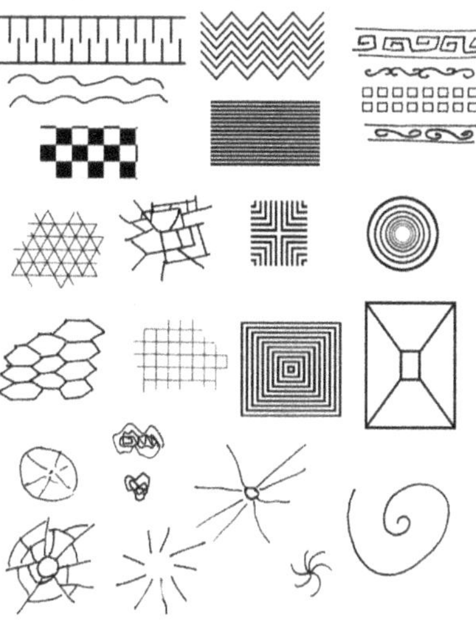

Fig. 1. A diagram showing form-constants derived from synesthesia/hallucinatory visions as discussed by Klüver and Dann. (© Michael Betancourt)

Michael Betancourt (artist, educator), 1230 22nd Street, Des Moines, IA 50311, U.S.A. E-mail: <michael@cinegraphic.net>.

decades earlier, but reified in the demands of "Business Art" for commercial viability understood as a symptom of aesthetic value or worth (the *economic* metaphor is explicit).

The dominance of these economic factors makes the complicity of earlier challenges to its hegemony apparent in their dependence on the marketplace, no matter what is being brought "to market." The crucial factor in this relationship is "to sell" which brings the art produced under the domain of business concerns—thus "Business Art." It places the artist in an untenable position: either accept the dominance of these relationships and their concomitant restrictions on action and possibility, or refuse them (and their economic, critical, and social supports) to become marginal. The issue is basic survival and continued possibilities for carrying on with what one does. Marginal is thus about displaced actions that continue with neither recognition nor official sanction. It is invisible.

The marginal position is the antithesis to what are variously acknowledged/identified positions (avant-garde, underground, experimental). It is emergent in the remainder (larger, less visible) created by any position that is recognized. The marginal is not, however, completely invisible—it is present, but to "see" it requires effort. Unlike the underground which requires a willful act of being hidden, oppositional—the marginal is simply ignored, unrecognized, because it does not match the demands being imposed by commerce and valorization.

Marginality is either and both a choice, and/or thrust upon: it is the "default" position for all artists until and unless they are subjects of valorization—accepted and incorporated by the demands of "Business Art" that affirm the established order and hierarchy of the status quo. The "marginal" is without clearly defined status in this cultural continuum. For the artist choosing marginality, it functions as a rejection of "Business Art"—but it also imposes the costs that valorization would otherwise pay and

Figure 1.3: Publication replaces exhibition in "Semiotics of the Moon as Fantasy and Destination" by Michael Betancourt

ARTIST'S ARTICLE

The Semiotics of the Moon as Fantasy and Destination

MICHAEL BETANCOURT

ABSTRACT

This essay surveys a 20-year period of the author's studio-based research into "spatial montage" and windowing, elaborating on his use of space imagery in a symbolic system describing the critique of fantasy::reality through symbols that are still used in the contemporary world—how the mythic dimensions of interpreting the "heavens" collide and contradict contemporary scientific interpretations. "Visionary" art is the dynamic focus, with the Moon as the central icon, providing a direct means for the author to consider ambiguities and complexities of symbolic transformation: earlier descriptions of heavens and Earth provide a visionary subtext to scientific exploration. The author considers himself a "revisionary" artist whose work engages the implicit semiotics of visionary film/visual music to problematize the pseudo-scientific theories found there.

I grew up in the 1970s fascinated by NASA's Apollo program; the Moon is a central image in my work. My collage novel, *Two Women and a Nightengale*, functions as a codex for my later, critical motion pictures. Mine is *not* the personal, "visionary" aesthetic based in the Romantic poetics described by film historian P. Adams Sitney, whose book *Visionary Film* linked the historical "experimental" or "avant-garde film" to earlier abstraction and transcendentalism:

> The preoccupations of the American avant-garde filmmakers coincide with those of our post-Romantic poets and Abstract Expressionist painters. Behind them lies a potent tradition of Romantic poetics. . . . The graphic cinema . . . continued its evolution with diminished force throughout the 1930s and 1940s. The coming of sound to film inspired several attempts to visualize music through cinematic abstractions and to synchronize visual rhythms to music [1].

Michael Betancourt (artist, historian, theorist, curator), Savannah, GA, U.S.A. Email: <michael@michaelbetancourt.com>.

See <www.mitpressjournals.org/toc/leon/48/5> for supplemental files associated with this issue.

Article Frontispiece. The final collage (no. 56), from *Two Women and a Nightengale* (1996–2004). (© Michael Betancourt/Artists Rights Society, NY)

Sitney's discussion of "absolute animation" (a.k.a. abstract film/visual music) identifies this transcendent tradition through discussions of artists such as Len Lye, John Whitney and Harry E. Smith. The visionary iconography Sitney discusses provides a way to address how our interpretations unconsciously reiterate earlier symbols through forms with multiple meanings (Fig. 1). My imagery invokes, then critiques through conceptual dissonance, Sitney's "visionary" tradition in both abstract art and visual music. These forms have a direct relationship to the esoteric ideas of Robert Fludd, whose "musical monochord" described a pseudo-scientific organization of the solar system through an analogy with Pythagorean musical intervals [2] (as Scott Montgomery's history of the Moon/lunar imagery noted, Pythagorean concerns have been linked to interpretations of the Moon since the 5th century BCE [3]). Whitney's theory of *digital harmony* shares this Pythagorean foundation for audiovisual synchronization [4]. My use of this tradition is semiotic and has become increasingly explicit: Glitches and technical errors/flaws act as signifiers for earlier conceptions of the same images. It enables the critique of pseudoscientific interpretations with contemporary ones: this contradictory reversibility of signs is inherent, an aspect I developed systematically in my film *Telemetry* (2003–2005).

Concepts of "Heavens and Earth" provide a visionary subtext to scientific exploration. Culture is a layering, where new ideas and interpretations form "sedimentary layers" over earlier ones, contradicting them, forming new meanings for old symbols. This principle organizes the historical material in my book *Two Women and a Nightengale* (1996–2004) whose imagery is a reference point for my later movies: *Telemetry* and the shorts *Aurora* (2001), *Illumination* (2001), *Contact Light* (2012) and *the Dark Rift* (2014). These ideas also emerge in my microwatt broadcast radio/video installation *Reception/Transmission* (2006). Unlike *Telemetry*, *Contact Light* and *the Dark Rift*, where the content of the movie directly addresses both space and the Moon, *Star Fish* (2012) and *Helios | Divine* (2013) both draw on this iconography, addressing the fantasy::reality dialectic posed by the Moon

 doi:10.1162/LEON_a_00919

support on the marginalized. Therefore the *choice* of marginality is a privileged choice of struggle (it is a privilege to be able to *select* marginal status). The problem this privilege presents is it can be rendered "mythic" when it should not be: the willful selection of marginality (choice) is to avoid the challenges of engaging valorization and remaining independent. Marginality is not independence, it is struggle at the boundary between economic viability and artistic visibility. Thus, other forms of support are required, leading to my proposition of "Research Art" as the contrary of "Business Art": an approach neither defined by patronage nor by marketplace exhibitions in the gallery-fair-museum network, but by the circulation through the horizontal planes of publication and documentation that exist independently of gallery and exhibition concerns.

"Research Art" thus occupies a specifically intellectual position in which the 'art object' becomes a vehicle for considerations traditionally restricted to the critic or historian. It is a proposition that can only exist *outside* the gallery-fair-museum network since it is not responsive to the economic demand that directs and determines "Business Art." Rather than being an academic art derived from adherence to *a priori* rules, its proposition as exploratory differentiates it from educational activity which must always strive to achieve immanent averageness in the propagation and internalization of criteria by students (affirming necessarily fixed values). In this regard, it is an extension of proposals and potentials initially developed by Conceptual Art, but which were radically subsumed by the marketplace as "Business Art" emerged as the dominant mode within the art world; the apparent repetitions and genres of commercial art derive from the conversion of historical avant-gardes into commodity-markers. "Research Art" is not a negation of the marketplace, nor its denial, but rather a parallel mode whose concerns, operations, and procedures do not intersect with valorization. It describes the complementary to industrial application—the disinterested exploration and development apart from commercial concerns. For "Research Art," the act of *publication* takes the place of *exhibition* [Figures 1.2 and

1.3]. Aesthetic production thus has two potential functions: *as-art* and *as-research* framed by a 'radically empirical' approach following William James' usage which assumes that reality is both continuous and non-dual, rejecting any separation between mind and body. (Even transcendence has a physical cue; this is what a "re-visionary aesthetic" means in practice.) This vehicle for cultural and critical exploration and theorization is discursive rather than programmatic. A self-consciously critical reflexivity demands careful attention to the distinction between intention and action, marking their separation as the ambiguous and ambivalent nature of the art work itself.

These theoretical concerns that guide this studio practice, and their articulation by the artist via publication, displace the aesthetic role of art criticism, establishing the Research Artist as a descendant of both the Conceptual Artists' and Situationalists' approach to art that cultivates a self-consciously theoretical relationship to studio practice, one in which aesthetics become history: an expression of contingent and arbitrary factors whose importance for working depends on the specific context invoked (cued) within/by the work itself. In place of the *a priori* fallacies of identity, intention, and biography, "Research Art" articulates experience and perception—the immanent encounter with the work. The art itself *is* the research, *is* the theory; however, this approach is radically empirical: it treats *all* subjectivities as interpreted products of specific, empirically present cues mediated by past experience. Knowledge derives from experience and encounter, but is mediated and informed by past experiences and the dispositive that contextualizes it. It creates distance between the expression and its expressiveness, allowing for more than a flat affect in the art itself. Investigation, modulation, and discourse become the intellectual concerns of studio-based research that may evoke a visceral response from its audience. It is not a matter of learning the discourse of others, but of critiquing all discourse directly through praxis.

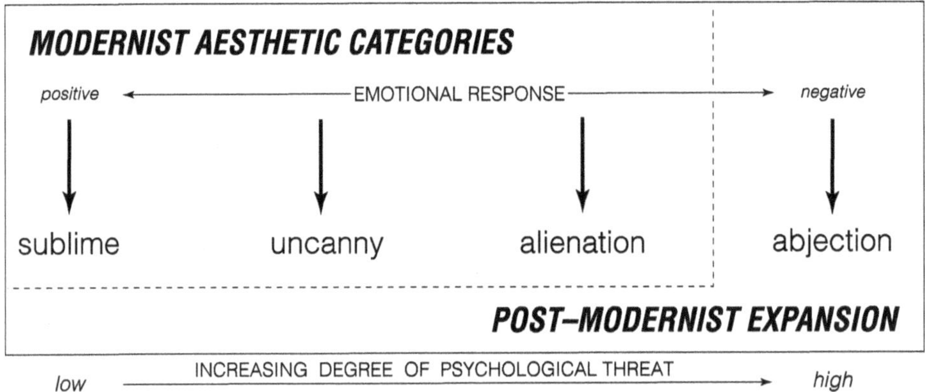

Figure 2.1: The ‘Uncanny’ is an affect theorized by the Modernist avant-garde as a critical mode. It is part of a spectrum of audience responses arranged by the degree of psychological threat they pose to the interpreter.

2
UNHEIMLICH GLITCH

The 'material function' cues the audience to interpret the "substance" of digital media *as-if* it is encoded,[15] yet it only becomes a critical engagement through a leap to an interpretation requiring more than just an acknowledgement of digital facture. Digital media is rendered for humans by an apparatus operating invisibly, continuously, and autonomously; however, interrupting the operation of the device is an insignificant challenge—lapses, drop-outs and other computer failures are commonplace, as are the slight "errors" (such as aliasing, bit-depth, gamma range, and object edges[16]) familiar from their use as *aesthetics* in media art. These transient electronic *mis*functions, "glitches," are ignored or elided from consideration, demonstrating the *aura of the digital* in operation: the ideally-conceived digital signal transcends its particular, immanent encounter (always imagined to be distinct from the perfection of the immaterial digital 'object') in a separation of digitality from its materiality that is a discursive fantasy of transcendent perfection. Conceiving the digital as independent of its presentation blocks the identification of materialist aesthetics essential to Glitch Art.[17] This diagnostic understanding of *glitch–as–noise* (a non-signifier) ends any further need for engagement, but also demonstrates that *all* interpretations are dependent on the low level identification that defines what requires consideration and attention: the audience's internalization of this rejection of materiality is the *aura of the digital* that creates basic difficulties of conceptualization by discursively displacing attention from the glitch into other registers—alluding to an *absent* original necessarily disengages from the encounter itself.

All interpretations proceed via two parallel, divergent modes that understand the immanent work either through the intratextual organization of its enunciations (the '*transparent mode*'), or via intertextual recognitions that create contextual analyses (the '*critical mode*'). These historical approaches employ distinct types of knowledge. Although both *transparent* and *critical modes* rely on the same cultural expertise, they are antithetical in elaboration. In shifting attention to the intertextual, the *critical mode* externalizes signification from the work being analyzed, potentially neglecting the intratextual order to address it as a product of quotations and conceptuality. Each mode's foundations relate to *how* they rely upon the audience's *a priori* knowledge and fluency:

> [**a**] The **transparent mode** is closely linked to the immanent encounter, an *intra*textual engagement that remains primarily fixed upon the enunciations and order arising from accepting its articulation.
>
> [**b**] The **critical mode** challenges immanent (*transparent*) elaborations through *inter*textual information *absent* from the immanent work—the critical identification of quotations, reiterations, and variations on schemas requires analysis, and relies on indexical recognition and lexical expertise for its application.

Critical modes arise from an autonomous decision to shift between 'accepting and embracing,' or 'challenging and expanding' both the contents and their articulation. The change from *intra*textual organization to *inter*textuality defines the Modernist "critical reading." Past experience and established expertise are fundamental to this approach—any insistence on the primacy of materiality over other factors such as contextuality is a concern with "purity" common to Formalist Modernism—a demonstration of an implicit aesthetic hierarchy that devalues the acceptance of *transparent* engagement. However, audiences typically employ aspects of both approaches simultaneously, engaging and anticipating critically in even the *transparent mode*; which approach (*intra*- versus *inter*-textual) dominates the primary analysis distinguishes between them—*both* require an active engagement. Attention to internal (intratextual) order is simultaneously a distinction between attention to aesthetics and formative order (*transparent*) and an intertextual concern with connecting a work to established iconography and lexical functions (*critical*).

The Modernist antipathy to the *transparent mode* arises in its apparently solipsistic attention to the internal ordering that is *not* a denial of externality; the consideration of morphology and structure (formative engagement) in the internal enunciation requires the same encultured lexicon of past experience to render interpretations coherent. Concerns with the "content" are the most apparent and typical demonstration of this internal primacy: the explanations offered teleologically justify the interpretation by the coherence it produces. In addressing the progression and organization of the immanent content, the *transparent mode* offers a formative description of meaning where the articulation itself is ignored in an embrace of what it presents. This concern for interpretive *transparency* can become a denial of context, aesthetics, and cultural significance.

When a glitch breaches or violates the expectations required by the *transparent mode* (does not provoke the discursive avoidance of the *aura of the digital*) it may have the same disruptive impact as the *Verfremdungseffekt* proposed by Bertolt Brecht (distancing or alienating effects, an uncanny sense of violated rules and conventional expectations). This "violation" acts as a cue to the audience: it identifies when a specifically *critical* rejection of *transparency* is appropriate, an implicitly aesthetic element, derived from formative relations and operating within (not against) familiar articulation:

> The audience can no longer have the illusion of being the unseen spectator at an event which is really taking place. [...] The artist's object is to appear strange and even surprising to the audience. He achieves this by looking strangely at himself and his work. As a result everything put forward by him has a touch of the amazing.

> Everyday things are thereby raised above the level of the obvious and automatic.[18]

Brecht's transformation/violation of expectations is neither automatic, nor is it an autonomous effect, but depends on *aesthetic* ruptures with the established expectations for both enunciation and articulation that challenge its Modernist origins by situating the audience centrally to this critical meaning: the *Verfremdungseffekt* is not just a formal effect that must originate in the unfamiliar, arising spontaneously and unexpectedly (thus corresponding to an *Unheimlich* experience[19]), but must derive from the audience's analysis—*both the expectations established in the work (transparent) and through its context (critical).* However, these interpretations cued by a formal device come as violations of the established order. Producing this cognitive shift requires more than the mere presence of a glitch: nothing automatically produces the essential defamiliarization—it is an aesthetic, thus formative, dimension of articulation. The use of glitches to produce this affect is *not* an issue of morphology and structure, but depends on context for its recognition.

The convergence between glitch and *Verfremdungseffekt* in the materiality of the digital—the renderings of encoded data—is complicated by the contradictory and paradoxical challenge of 'unmasking artifice' implicit in Brecht's proposal of the *Verfremdungseffekt.*[20] The revelation of contingency and artifice for interpretation becomes an *Unheimlich* disabusal of anticipated progression, morphology, and structure [Figure 2.2]. The disruptive effect that "shocks" depends specifically on a *transparent* acceptance of the internal articulation, one that is readily challenged by any *un*anticipated deviation from the expected ordering.[21] Aesthetic apprehension of materiality and physical form is an awareness of *both transparent* and *critical modes* as contingencies created by specifically social, economic, and political factors that are unconscious. Unlike critical interpretation, the "defamiliarized" is an encounter with alterity that renders existing orders as ambiguous potentials within a range of possibilities. This experience explicates the

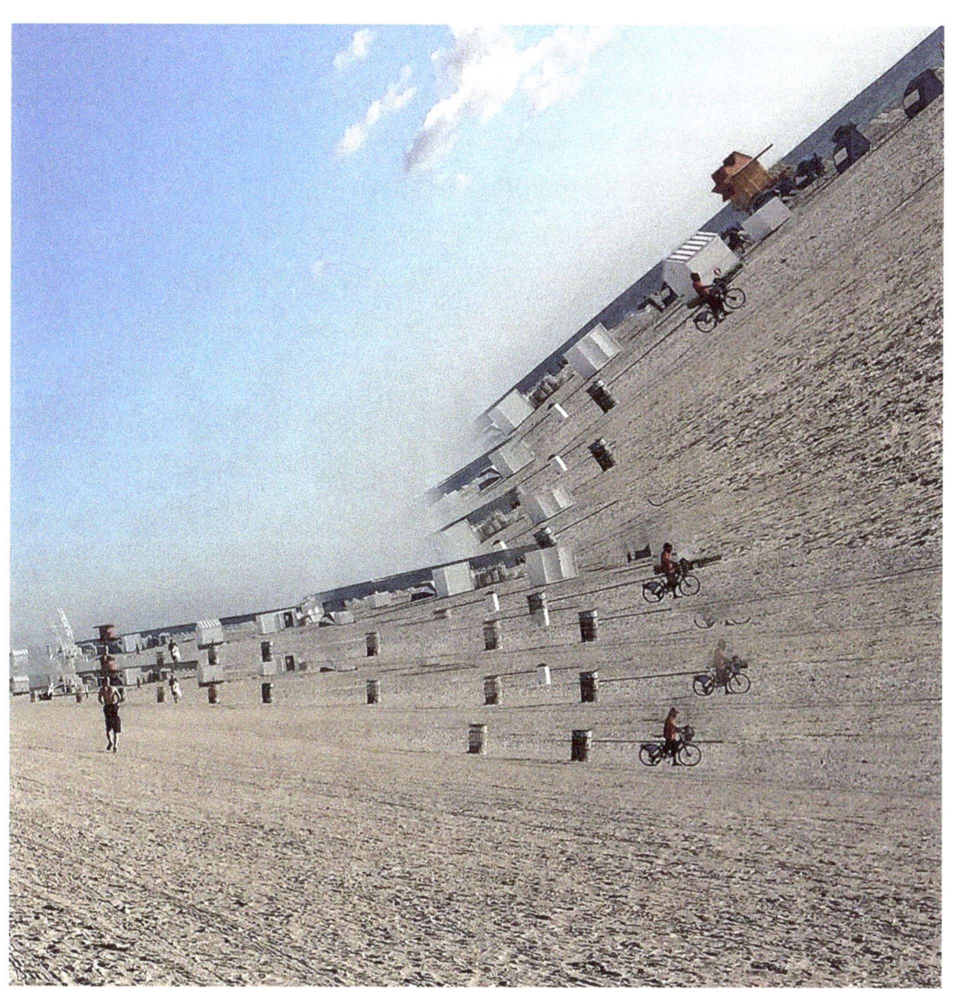

Figure 2.2: *Instaglitch_16908426_260348597753145_8598616421712265216_n*
copyright © 2017 Michael Betancourt
courtesy Artists Rights Society (ARS)

source of the *Unheimlich*—a conversion from the familiar, comfortable relations to a threatening and capricious modality where articulation becomes a self-evident force structuring and creating an artificial, imposed order.

Understanding eruptions of materiality as an autonomous interference with the (rejected) "transparency" of Modernist aesthetics identifies how the *Verfremdungseffekt* depends on conceiving the audience as *passive,* as needing to be 'shocked' out of their complicity.[22] The historical, over-determined protocols for *Verfremdungseffekt* are not necessarily productive of defamiliarization. All the historical techniques for cueing this 'critical rupture' have become a commonplace element in *transparent* articulation, in the morphology and structure of both narrative and non-narrative works:

[1] **direct address** to the audience

[2] the quotation or disruptive **non-sequitur**

[3] **breaching** the "fourth wall"

[4] works with **critical content**

[5] drawing attention to the **artifice**

[6] the intrusion of "**noise**" that disrupts the work (typically ignorable as external to the media)

Each aesthetic protocol stands apart from the familiar *transparent mode*, yet can be assimilated back to it—a transformation from *Unheimlich* to *Heimlich*, alienation to everydayness—giving their roles an ambivalent character. All six aesthetic techniques are well-known and familiar, yet only the responses to [5] and [6] do not necessarily entail the return to an uncritical, *transparent* engagement. Brecht's materialist defamiliarization attacks denotation and the primary identification of content, thus cannot be reinscribed back into *transparency*; [5] and [6] must be expelled as insignificant (noise) to reassert the familiar order.

However, the *Unheimlich glitch* arises from an emergent recognition of contingency—shifting from material process to the identification/acknowledgement of its semiotic role: it depends on cues provided by specific morphologies and structures. The transition between *transparent* and *critical modes* always has an intertextual character: the audience identifies aesthetic (formative) features as directing their locus of attention towards another level of complexity (*poesis*) *not* apparent in the denotation, but arising from their past experiences and established expertise with the serial nature of interpretation.[23] The change from immanence to experience is an autonomous decision. Yet what is of interest are those situations where this changed approach can be considered a specific feature cued by an aesthetic *attribute,* rather than simply a decision made independently by the audience;[24] however, this recognition of a "critical aesthetics" remains a distinction that must be identified by the audience.

The *aura of the digital* reverses all these unmaskings by discursively returning to the *Heimlich*, a counter-revelatory engagement which precisely undermines any potential ruptures. The term, *Heimlich*—"at homeness"—forecloses on potential opposition: the safety and familiarity of an unquestioned and expected order is precisely appropriate.[25] The *aura of the digital* protects *transparent* analysis by maintaining the invisibility of articulations and the fantasy of transcendent digital media perfection, separate from the mere materiality of its presentation. The challenge offered by defamiliarization of *Verfremdungseffekt* transforms this transcendence into an *Unheimlich* encounter with an alien and ambivalent technical product, as in my movie *Contact Light* (2012), my movie serial *Going Somewhere* (2015–2018), and the 2,600 still images in the *Instaglitch project* (2016–2020) made by inducing glitches in the *Instagram* app on an *iPhone*, all demonstrate. To return to a familiar and stable 'transparency' requires a disavowal of the glitch's violations: recoding it as either irrelevant (noise), or as a material sign for the technology that can be accepted as a novel, but syntactical part of enunciation, much like fades, dissolves, and other graphic, visual effects that serve as transitions or markers.

"Critical glitches" require a specific identification of signification at more than just the immanent level of encounter, "signaled" to the audience by formative elements of digital media apart from their materiality. The most apparent 'provocations' arise in the thoroughly and completely glitched work where the "technical failures" are not occasional interruptions, but the entire substance of what appears—this completeness gives these glitches a superficial identification as an 'inherent' criticality. Theoretical analysis that specifies a set of factors (cues) *for* criticality is the problem. The assumption that materiality is a signifier of criticality (the heritage of Modernism) mistakes the conclusion for its syllogism; errors of this type lead to the false belief in *inherent* meanings—thus creating precisely the same *transparent* engagement challenged by the *critical mode*. This modal overlap makes the aesthetics of defamiliarized articulation neither representative of general rules, nor the unique properties of singular works. Although derived from *formative* cues, those cues are neither predetermined, nor predefined. They reflect the role of past experience in framing analysis, a demonstration of the ambivalence of all signification processes: signs are neither necessarily critical, nor essentially non-critical, but are defined through their use/re-use within a specific work (*context*). The assimilation of glitches in/as a conventional demonstration of materiality is a reflection of the audience's autonomous facility to adapt, recoding novel variances/ruptures as structural and expected features—their *aesthetic* nature returns any novel morphology to the realm of the *Heimlich,* and so denies any disruption it might produce. This recoding of materiality as conventional "criticality" precisely shifts from defamiliarized to familiar, a transition that does not preclude an additional *critical* semiosis, but does make the ambivalent role of articulation and the analytic reversibility of glitches apparent. Instability is essential to these shifts. Only works that have established expectations and/or internalized codes offer the potential for posing any disruptive or transformative 'shock'—defamiliarization of their enunciation—by creating a mismatch between their articulation and its interpretation.

Critical Cues

Aesthetic qualia apparent in the morphology and structure of past works have a gravitational effect on novel and alienated forms, drawing them back towards familiar and established frameworks. The ambivalent challenge of Brecht's *Verfremdungseffekt* therefore creates a conceptual problem by conceiving of its impacts as simultaneously liberating and capturing its audience,[26] which is resolved if these potentials are not considered antithetical but as an ambivalence that ungrounds established expertise. The sudden violation of normalcy-bias in audience engagements (even for the *critical modes* there are "transparent" procedures) has a history of *assumed* criticality apparent in Brecht's Marxist analysis; yet the problem is not *a priori* meaning. While acknowledging the contingency and the artificiality of interpretations serves an important clarifying function in understanding the development of *critical modes* for Glitch Art—the revenants of historical Modernist aesthetics are still powerful distractions—these disruptive 'shocks' are the unanticipated transformation of familiar cues to interpret *as-if* "encoded." The *Unheimlich* eruption precisely challenges these expectations. A frission between the anticipated order and the immediate encounter violates the established, intratextual aesthetic—making the artificial and contingent nature of *transparency* apparent. This normative interpretation further collides with the *critical modes* offered/established in/by past experience, leaving both in question: the defamiliarized rupture demonstrated by the *Verfremdungseffekt.*

The teleological and totalizing force of Modernist aesthetic forms (and their ruptures)—now unquestionably historical—remain as implicit constraints on new work; the six familiar protocols for *Verfremdungseffekt* have an extended reach into the Contemporary. Digital technologies offer potentials distinct from the stable and discrete media-forms employed in the twentieth century; the emergent structures of post-digitality undermine oppositions of *realism::abstraction* and *narrative::non-narrative*. Digital imaging reveals these separate, established potentials as existing in dynamic ranges where the familiar positions are points of maximum difference, with a continuum of intermediary positions being the substance of actual experience and encounter. Post-digitality challenges historical media by making the fluidity of these ranges central to its aesthetics, i.e. in the use of glitches and related processes. The contingency of interpretation for basic issues of denotation and connotation emerges in the digital articulation. The instability of glitched, processed, and compressed materials engages fundamentals of perception, thus making the audience's initial and proximate decisions to resolve ambivalent denotation apparent in their higher level comprehensions. These playful possibilities are always paradoxical, challenging the revenant Modernist aesthetics that continue to inform digital media. Mutually exclusive positions establish impossible alternatives, identified by points of maximum difference—which simultaneously lie within the same range—that *all* remain true, revealing how enculturation establishes articulation: lower-level interpretations are the foundation for the higher-levels, a recursive progression from perception to interpretation. Art composed *entirely* from glitches superficially normalize their glitched materials, re-imposing the *transparent* order, even if the instability of the representational and ontological 'content' of glitches does shift the historical dynamic of photographic realism identified in the range of realist denotation defined by *naturalism::stylization.* Distinguishing post-digital glitched imagery from traditional realism allows it simultaneously to be graphically patterned abstraction and familiar representation, an ambivalent doubling that undermines stable interpretations.

Defamiliarization arises in encounters where established interpretive schemas suggest contradictory (if not mutually exclusive) understandings of a singular subject. For example, the ambivalences of abstraction/realism, glitch/not-glitched, and narrative/non-narrative can be a starting point for this defamiliarization process: these ruptures are specifically aesthetic (*formative*), derived from an ambiguous morphology and structure that destabilizes established categories—an uncertain intertextuality that cannot conclude the encounter. Past experience misleadingly invokes familiar tropes—such as paranarratives[27] employing only the rudimentary essentials for their recognition, relying on their audiences to supply the significant links and organization—the apparent *fabula* (plot). These returns to *transparency* justify their interpretations by the result—a circularity of cause and effect that distinguishes the paranarrative from other, more familiar, complete, and self-sufficient narrative forms. It is parasitical on established interpretations without expanding on them, making the paranarrative an ambivalent enunciative device, as both *Going Somewhere* and *Contact Light* demonstrate. However, the recognition of a paranarrative requires a familiarity with its intertextual *Ur*-source; an insufficient knowledge may result in a paranarrative that remains ambivalent or entirely unidentified. This dynamic between *recognition::ignorance* makes the serial dimensions of all interpretive constructs obvious. Audiences must identify the absent-schema to understand the paranarrative, as semiotician Umberto Eco notes in "Interpreting Serials":

> It must achieve a dialectic between order and novelty, in other words between schema and innovation. This dialectic must be perceived by the consumer, who must grasp not only the contents of the message, but also the way in which the message transmits those contents.[28]

By drawing from past experience to understand the immanent order, the audience must use their already existing lexical expertise to decode/invent its implied (but absent) connections. Paranarratives are a synthesis of immanent organization and audience anticipation and recognition, generating coherence equally from the emergent convergences and differences with the intertextual schema. This fusion of externalities does not necessarily render a critical result: the progression remains linked to the *transparent mode*. While the quotation of a particular use directs attention to the absent source, only a return to the immediate presentation makes it coherent, an affirmation of its *internal* organization. A quote recognized does not eliminate the *transparent* analysis of an immanent work, it complicates it. The morphology thus recognized in *Verfremdungseffekt* becomes a structural principle that deepens without challenging the meaning '*transparently*' offered by its own invisible articulations. The identification of "critical" glitches is thus a direct reflection of *who* the audience is.[29] The complex instabilities of glitched materials enable mutually exclusive interpretations to emerge for the *same* work, demonstrating the audience's particular engagement and lexical fluency is the causal factor in/for producing critical media, rather than any technique that may be commonly employed to 'cue' that interpretation.

The 'Defamiliar Consciousness'

The critical potential for the *Unheimlich glitch* to exceed its Modernist foundations cannot be over-emphasized. It is precisely a product of post-digitality violating the established "ontological" order of images—the differentiation between Modernist conceptions of medium-specificity and the convergent break-down of those boundaries by computer technology—coupled with the expansion of its dispositive by the emergent identifications of ambivalent meaning posed by a mobile articulation. The specifically *Unheimlich* dimensions of digital materiality for ontological and indexical conceptions of photographic images (as demonstrated by the glitch) resides in displacements of established lexical expertise that become apparent in defamiliarization. It is not the cues of mere materiality, but their role in interpretation that is essential. Conceptions of the *medium* mask the ideological and lexical dimensions of post-digital challenges, effectively emphasizing a Modernist aesthetic of materiality (to the exclusion of both *critical* and *transparent modes'* adaptation to its now historical challenges) that maintains the familiar order against disruption.

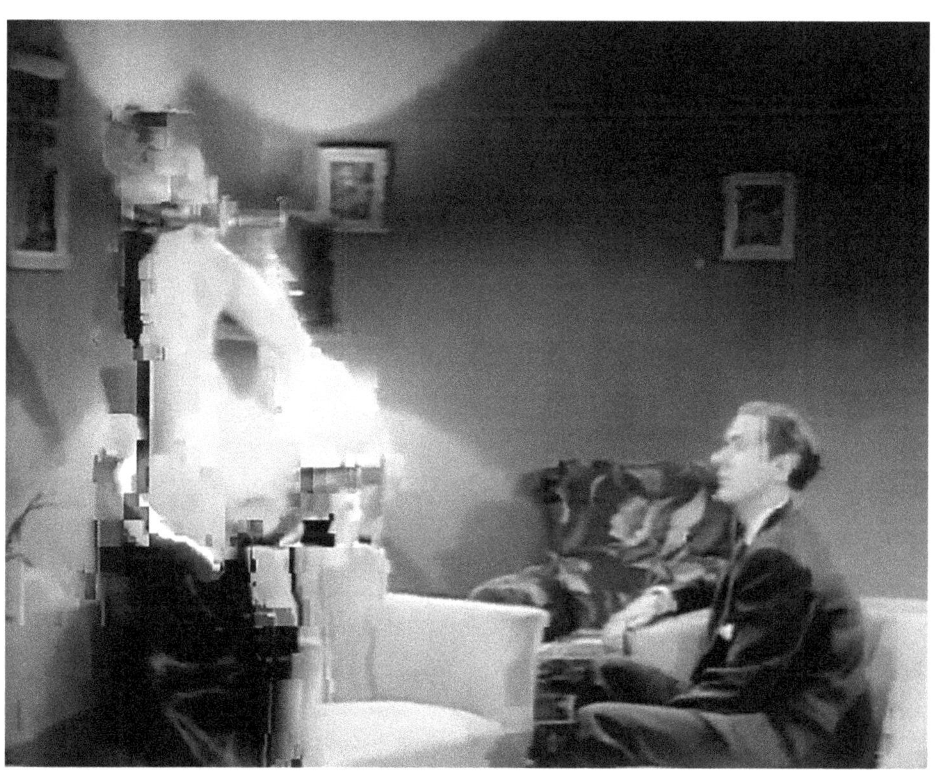

Figure 2.3: *Noir Disappearance*
copyright © 2016 Michael Betancourt
courtesy Artists Rights Society (ARS)

Experience is the substance of motion pictures; the modulation of the encounter is central to its articulation. This chain of connections is explicit. Constructing a critical media depends on shifting the audience's attention to this momentary, immediate construction reflexively. Because enunciation arises from the identifications of articulation, the use of glitch does not change this formative role for experience, even if the materials being articulated proceed in atypical ways different from those of historical orders: the *transparent mode* is flexible, accommodating the specific (immanent) morphology, whether it is organized in familiar or unfamiliar ways. The *Unheimlich* is a *discursive* intepretive response produced by specific situations:

[**a**] The **novelty** of the morphology.

[**b**] The emergent **structure** the morphology produces.

The challenges posed by [a] will fade with familiarity, while [b] depends on the lexical organization of internal cues, rather than the novelty of their form. Both converge on the same formative protocols, employing them in distinct, diverging ways. Glitch Art depends morphologies and structures particular to the capabilities of digital systems in ways that transform the assumptions of historical media into one set of conventional uses, offering alternatives that challenge the ontological claim of a link between the imagery shown on-screen and the mechanism of its production, potentially alienating these Modernist foundations.

Resolving the problem of the *Heimlich* and the *Unheimlich* is internal to the *aura of the digital*. In eliding the disruptive aspects posed by digital technology, this return to *transparency* simultaneously makes its rupture into a cue "liberating" re-engagement with the materiality of digital facture: the generative and autonomous production becomes apparent as a screen articulating the encounter. Drawing attention to the physically situated audience in relation to this presentation reverses the *aura of the digital*, an unmasking of technical operations that cues a *critical* response through its delayed re-articulation as a 'material function' producing the enunciated contents.

Although the historical type of critical-working that Brecht's *Verfremdungseffekt* offers reflects a Marxist dialectics, the defamiliarized dimension it suggests opens away from either the fixed duality of class and political economy, or a heightened consciousness 'shocked' into being critical. This evasion is more than a minor ambivalence or contradiction,[30] it is the essence of its *critical* potential, and is what gives defamiliarization an after-life apart from historically Modernist and Marxist uses—themselves an attempt at a redirection of the *Unheimlich* disruption into a specific and limited *a priori* "critical" framework. Shifting between familiar/defamiliar does not concern the thing perceived, but the perceiving-process: it undermines and counters any particular function (use) for defamiliarization, linking it to earlier conceptions of the sublime (and transcendence) already established in the term "unheimlich" (uncanny), and pointing towards the discursive potentials of alienation and abjection that accentuate its disruptive aspects [Figure 2.1]. This 'defamiliarization protocol' subverts any and all established systems: an identifier for the revelation of artifice, the '*critical*' engagement offered is categorically distinct from the *critical mode*. It is an activity that produces knowledge-awareness of contingency—and so of alternatives as equally possible and valid.

The role of discursive intertextuality becomes apparent when audiences must confront their *a priori* beliefs as determinate, constructive functions that depend on their tentative imposition of a causal order reflexively constructed from past experience and prior knowledge. *Critical glitches* act as a decoding matrix, allowing the audience to suddenly perceive the meaning, but without the fixity and stability common to transparent analysis. This awareness of meaning defined in advance and left unquestioned makes the sudden insight it creates into a metastable, transient contingency revealing the illusion of a singular order; thus, the glitch comes into consciousness *only* when the audience's imposed order becomes a factor of its interpretation—reiterating the role of defamiliarization in the *Unheimlich* (uncanny) and *Verfremdungseffekt*.

This 'defamiliar consciousness' does not become *critical* through recourse to a predetermined analytic protocol, instead emerging from the awareness fostered by the contingency of that process. These results, while related to the Modernist aesthetics of Brecht's *Verfremdungseffekt,* will always exceed them: the *Unheimlich* is a transitive experience, one that morphs over time, remaining the same *and* continuously changing to meet the demands of a novel situation beyond his Modernist/ Marxist dialectic. Yet *defamiliarization* remains constant: without the violation of expectations (whatever they have become) the rupture does not take place—how this process escapes containment is neither an historical protocol, nor isolated within a particular aesthetic (such as the glitch), nor even the particular framework of Marxism. Any destabilization of established signifiers will necessarily challenge whatever comfortable assumptions make them appear familiar and unquestionable. The *Unheimlich* thus adapts to novel situations, taking on appropriate formative characteristics that identify the margins and resentiments of the status quo, bringing their contingency back into conscious awareness—this protean shifting is definitional. The defamiliarized is an excluded and uncomfortable limit that always lies at the margin whose rejection and displacement in Contemporary media (erasure by the *aura of the digital*) maintains the coherent, existing order; returns of the excluded and elided ungrounded accepted orders because they reveal their imposed nature as artifice. Escaping the superficial entanglement of Modernist concerns with the *Unheimlich* reflects the challenges posed for Glitch Art as a model cueing a *critical mode* generally—it is a model for initiating a self-referential encounter for the audience—resulting in a 'criticality' that challenges both *critical* and *transparent modes*' totalizing and teleological analyses. The challenge for critical media is to escape from the confines and limitations of Post- and Modernist "radical challenge" to propose something *else* that begins when the experiential encounter becomes central to articulation.

3
Discursive Transcendence

Central to my critique of digital capitalism is an analytic 'tool,' the *aura of the digital*, which has a broad range of implications that are especially visible as a sociological and economic myopia that denies the costs, physicality, and material nature of computer technology.[31] But as an aesthetic concept, the "aura of the digital" identifies a transcendent value implicit in viewing the immaterial digital file as the "true" work; this distinction between the immaterial file and its physical presentation creates a 'discursive aesthetic' that matches the denial of the gallery/exhibition context in Modernist aesthetics,[32] apparent in how 'technical fluency' idealizes the source file. The *aura of the digital's* refusal of materiality produces this deference—ignoring not only the capital, labor, and resources digital technology consumes, but also refusing to consider the immanent display or presentation of digital files.[33] The association of *mis*functions with a transcendental signified (the 'discursive aesthetic') derive from this shift away from an immanent encounter to a consideration of the absent original—the denial of immediate experience identified by the *aura of the digital*. 'Discursive aesthetics' arise in the mundane, everyday encounters that displace concerns with the physicality of digital media to declare all physical manifestations and all presentations (especially glitched ones) to be imperfect replicas of a perfect (virtual) original, the data file. This *transparent* identification acts to instrumentalize the 'transcendent values'[34] that derive from the (formerly avant-garde) materialist aesthetics that have come to dominate media art since the 1970s.[35] Treating 'media' *as-art* began in the Modernist concern with "purity" that defined each medium independently of all other media,[36] a tradition that continues in Glitch Art precisely because it exploits the audience's capacity to view 'errors' as aesthetic objects[37] linked to the digital medium,[38] (leading to their simulation[39] as purely formal recognitions of technology itself.[40]) Materialist aesthetics enable *mis*function and all forms of technical error to become a transcendent expression of primordial, metaphysical content[41] because idealizing the data file informs recognizing a glitch. Ironically, it conceives variability-in-display as symptomatic of an idealized work that can never appear; deferral to the unglitched discursively skirts the 'glitch' to consider its aesthetic features as variations around the perfectly hypothetical "original." This concern for an absent-but-essential 'source' that is unglitched[42] produces a circular assertion that reinforces understanding the data file as the only 'real' work, ignoring the errors themselves as *noise*.[43] These are cyclic, tautological relationships, self-reinforcing and replicating.

The *aura of the digital* informs 'technical fluency' as the *transparent* approach to media concerned with the "content," but which denigrates the particulars of its actual, immanent encounter. This act creates the expectations that digital glitches are a transitory problem with the display, not a feature of the work: it marks the data file as a *literal* value more complete, more perfect, more reliable than any physical presentation—an imaginary perfection residing with the datastream that contrasts with the immanent products of its implementation for a human audience—reifying the glitch as a *mal*function to ignore.[44] Considering the data file as the real, inviolate art object manifests the 'discursive aesthetic' as a pseudo-Platonic idealization[45] where digital perfection can only be apprehended through noise, breach, and breakdown (i.e. *experientially*).[46]

The iconography of visual glitches—characteristic streaks, flows, and fragmentation[47]—arise from technical variances in either the data itself or the decoding codec[48] since digital images do not store pictorial data: they are generative products of algorithms that compress and decompress instrumental instructions to

---

Figure 3.1: Examples of technical breakdowns as diagnostics in the 1949 repair handbook *RCA Television Pict-O-Guide: An Aid to TV Troubleshooting, Volume 1* by John R. Meagher.

RCA Television PICT-O-GUIDE

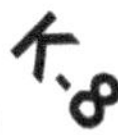

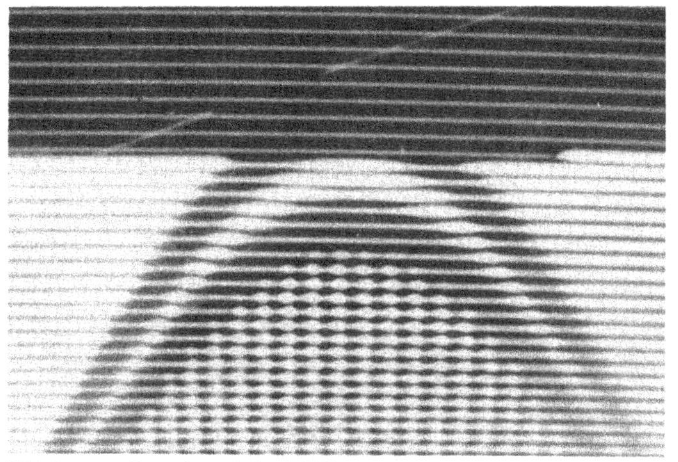

This is a small section of the **WFIL** test pattern spread out vertically to show the scanning-line structure, with brightness advanced to make the lines thicker than usual. Read K-8 to K-8b.

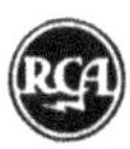

RCA Television PICT-O-GUIDE

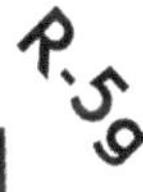

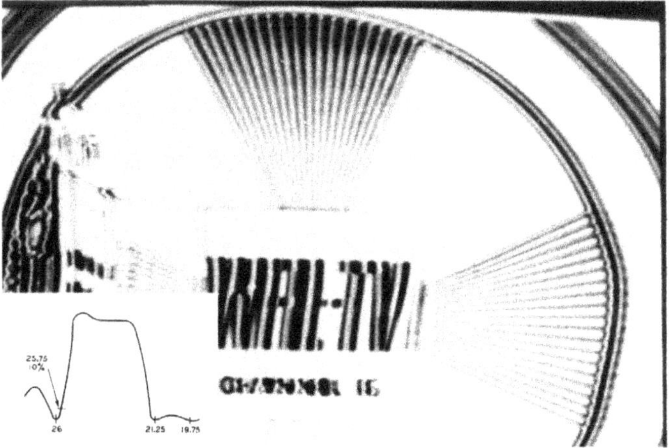

Picture carrier at 10%. Poor low-frequency response indicated by weak horizontal wedge. Also causes poor sync, poor blanking, and poor signal-to-noise ratio. Read R-5 to R-5h.

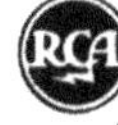

render their "contents" human-readable.[49] Identifying these contents as showing a "glitch" ratifies the proposal that the immanent digital display is not 'the image' itself, but merely one instance of a vastly reproducible and replicable work. A "glitch" is this normal process producing unanticipated results that are often recoded as cues for 'authenticity' and 'cultural value.'[50] Understanding their identification *as-glitch* thus poses several potential interpretations for media art:

> [**a**] Diagnostic interpretations of *mal*function as a **symptom** aspires to being an ontological demonstration of technical failure [Figure 3.1], potentially requiring some response from the audience, thus ending their interpretive engagement with the depiction as-being the *thing–in–itself.* No further semiosis is possible since, in being reality, it precludes symbolic articulation.
>
> [**b**] Symbolic identifications of *mis*function, a **reflexive** claim to *being-factual,* (i.e. as "historical testimony" or proof of authenticity), articulates meaning through the encultured structures of *realism* as a *naturalistic* "veil of nature" that limits them to being a *statement about the image's materiality,* as with simulations of degraded footage that denotes *mal*function, but requires no response—it is not a symptom of breakdown, but an element of *découpage* distinct from the diegetic space on-screen.
>
> [**c**] Narrative identification of *failure-as-failure*, **representing** a "breakdown" as a *causal* product of events depicted—as an element of the diegesis incorporated and explained through the narrative functions of *sujet* and *fabula.*
>
> [**d**] *Failure-as-aesthetic* defines an **artifact** presented and used expressively as a method to cue and identify

> *poeisis,* which demands these "material markers" receive consideration for their specific audio-visual properties.

Contemporary technology offers a range of telescreen displays, (cellphone, computer, television, movie theater, et. al.), but the constancy of the 'discursive aesthetic' across these displays shows how the digital file is assumed to be adaptable, mutable, incorruptible—although any particular display may have problems, those errors are believed to be proximate to its exhibition, not integral to the work [a]. However, when glitch iconography becomes a diagnostic for "materiality," it reifies the transcendence of the 'discursive aesthetic,' paradoxically, in the glitches themselves. These disruptions require an absent, perfect image that hypothetically would otherwise appear: Glitch Art develops these conventions of 'materiality' into an expressive element, "flirting" with disaster to consider them as *errors-which-are-not-errors,* showing the symptoms (diagnostic) for a digital breakdown [a] without being an actual failure [b, c, d]. Digital media depend on the instrumental separation between 'image display' and the 'instrumental instructions' of data, a difference in form that distinguishes the machine-generated file from its human-readable presentation.

Digital art develops from a categorically different type of immateriality than that of analogue electronics since the computational nature of all digital art separates the historical unification of 'image and signal,' as in video processing. The analogue signal directly relates to its display, but the digital's independence from its display is inherent: code does not "contain" the work, it generates it. The 'discursive aesthetic' emerges from how these technical images originate in a *datastream* (information contained by/in the digital file) that is the source of the immanent presentation, a technical foundation that authorizes understanding its apprehension as the *transformation* of this hidden 'source.' It modulates the experience of the work. This displacement is a refusal of the immanent encounter that is also a refusal of the physicality of digital files: the aesthetics it identifies can only become apparent through the potentially self-referential nature of limina, such as the glitch, creating the fallacy[51] that a glitch is an automatically or inherently 'political' gesture.[52] When understood in these terms, the iconography of glitches apparent in [d] *failure-as-aesthetic* become symptoms of a discursive shift, the *aura of the digital*. Only abnormal circumstances draws the *mis*functions produced by 'errors' into consciousness as a 'parting the veil' on the ideology of these computational operations. The *transparent* engagement via the *aura of the digital* that apprehends the diagnostic significance of glitches may make note of their presence, but this identification is not necessarily critical—only a conscious choice by the audience, one that may be cued by the contextual use of a glitch, can become critical; however, the 'discursive aesthetic' renders a diagnostic of what "remains" in the glitched image as indicative of what is missing (the 'source'), neutralizing its critical potential.

Images transformed by circulation through a variety of displays and presentations identify these 'discursive aesthetics' via their 'transparent' engagement within normative readings only concerned with their "contents," rather than the expression itself: thus the intransigence of glitches is not a disruption and effacement of the idealized original, but instead invokes it via the audience's rejection of material concerns. Understanding the (glitched) physical presentation derives from the viewer's 'technical fluency' that defines an ambivalent *reverie* whose *transparency* also denies *critical* engagement, even though it can also act as a cue for one: glitch iconography requires a change in consciousness to be a revelation of computational processing. The shift to *being-critical* is an autonomous choice by the audience, cued *a priori* by past experience with media art that conventionally identifies *when* this change in mode may be appropriate; thus cueing is not a critical significance, merely the recognition of contextual *uses* of glitches that suggest it is appropriate to interpret *as-if* the work has a *critical* encoding. These cues are all easily identified as instances of [d] *failure-as-aesthetic*, however their *criticality* depends on their specific use within that identification—it is a product of the meaning of the work, rather than the presence of glitches.

But the transcendence posed by the 'discursive aesthetic' precisely blocks any self-conscious consideration, even in works cueing *poeisis,* because the *critical* apprehension of the glitch requires more than just the aesthetic appreciation of this iconography as expressive. Considering *mis*function as poetic reveals this engagement lies in the apparent and assumed transformations enacted upon idealized sources: the "error, recognized" establishes the glitched image as a "quotation" of its unbroken self, a flawed copy. These typical relations define their iconography as features of a "glitch aesthetic" that acts transparently, drawing attention not to a critical meaning, but to the transcendence instrumentally contained in/as the datastream itself—it is an ironic cypher for an impossible perfection and authenticity of expression. As with the *Verfremdungseffekt,* these significances neither challenge nor critique the *transparent* relationships they depend on, even if their use articulates a formally self-conscious and reflexive stylistic gesture.

The *Instaglitch* series

My *Instaglitch* project exploits the aberrant and *unheimlich* results of image handling and processing by the *Instagram* photosharing app to derive novel examples of Glitch Art from the faults inherent to the *iPhone* system [Figure 3.2]. This project uses these inconsistencies as a mechanism for aesthetic creation that provides evidence for the fantasy of control that the "walled garden" of apps create. The development of the *Instaglitch* offers a counter to this hegemonic ideology via a studio practice that exploits the *Instagram* app's very limited 'degrees of freedom' without altering the app itself or employing less restrictive software. These works are examples of how repeated processing and 'filtering' of the same image within the same system—a feedback loop—magnifies the instabilities inherent in its operations. The 2,600 works in this series of static images demonstrates programmatic failures that are masked by

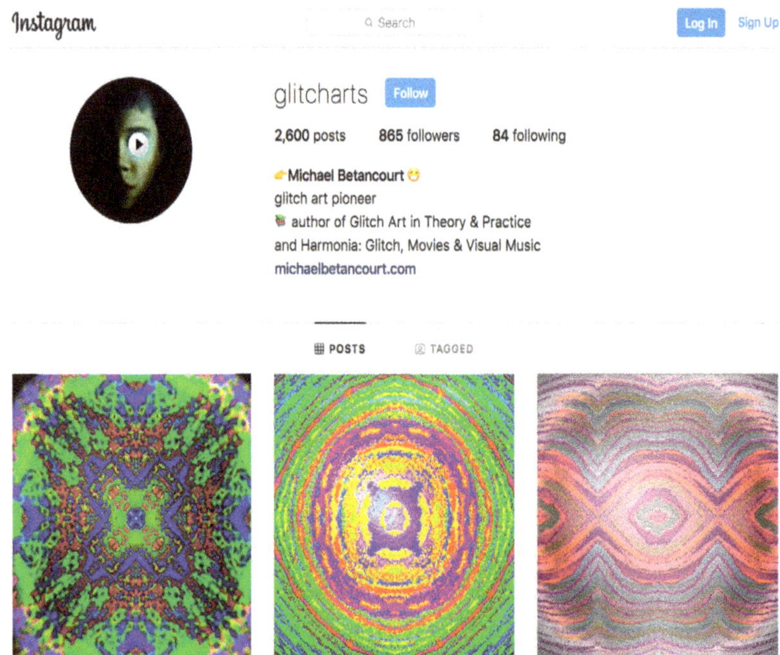

Figure 3.2: The *Instagram* account (***@glitcharts***) used to generate and post the images in the project.

---

its normal use, but are systemic instabilities—their identification allowed me to generate works by manipulating their impacts on a blank (white) image. These glitch images are a product of the noise and artifacts created by the software's typical operation. This exploit of faults and breakdowns is antithetical to the 'discursive aesthetic' and the glitch's typical role as either [c] *failure-as-failure* or [d] *failure-as-aesthetic*. There is no "original" that these works can even hypothetically reference.

There is no damage in an *Instaglitch*: it is exactly as it should be, a product of the intersection between the digital system (the app) and the demands being made by the user (me). In the highly regimented and limited freedom granted by "apps" on tablets and cellphones, the design of the system itself controls and constrains the actions of its users in ways that more traditional digital computers do not—evidence for the fantasy of control they produce—making this aesthetic research into its marginal

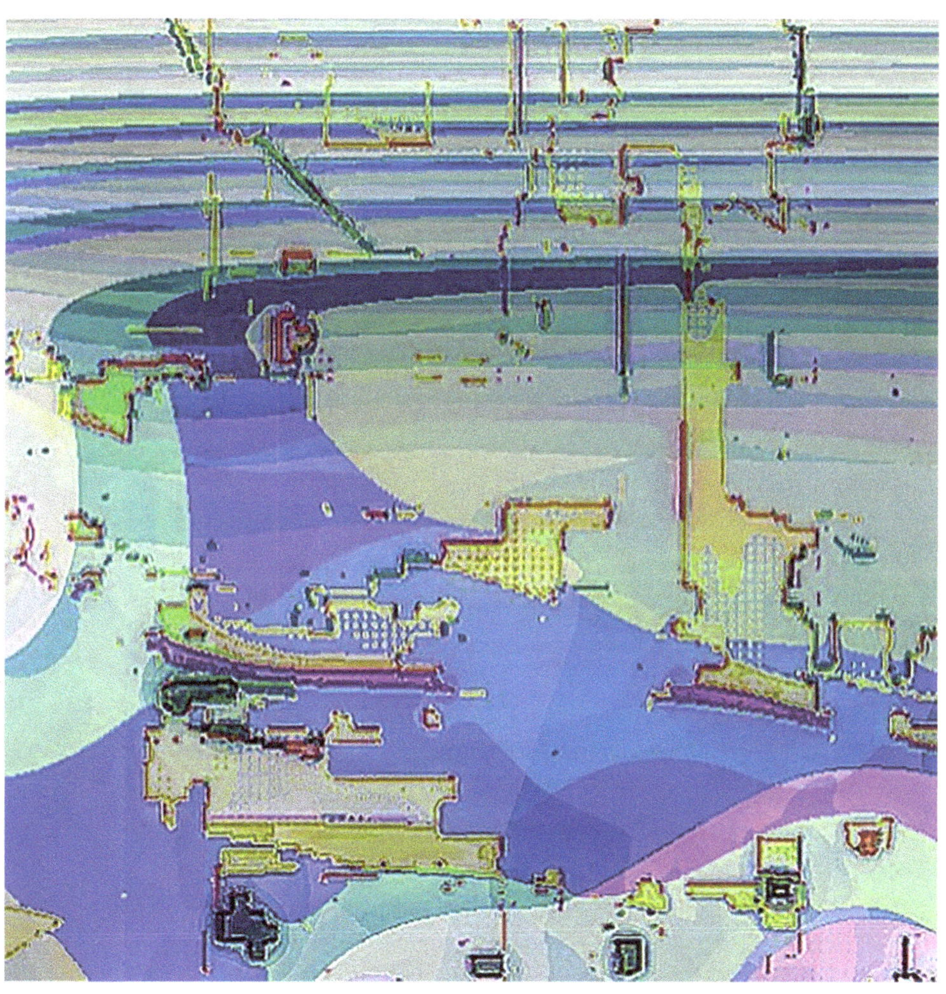

Figure 3.3: *Instaglitch_25005797_1729050553773029_7451705676591529984_n*
copyright © 2017 Michael Betancourt
courtesy Artists Rights Society (ARS)

aesthetic capacity critically germane. The limitations of the *Instagram* system are precisely the point: being a commercial, populist system, it was expressly designed to minimize the capacity for the kinds of glitch imagery and exploit I used. The development of the *Instaglitch* offers an aesthetic revelation of this hegemonic system.

The *Instaglitch* demonstrates the fluid nature of what is considered "damage" or "noise" in the system versus its identification as/with expressive works.[53] This series reveals the illusion that digital systems are fully controllable, that the degrees of freedom[54] they offer their users can be entirely limited and all the potential applications accounted for in advance of their use: it unmasks the illusion that digital systems are fully controllable.

Unlike the more common software bugs or malicious exploits of security flaws in digital systems, the *Instaglitch* offers an alternative conception of *mis*function as neither negative, nor undesirable. The superficial familiarity and recognizable suggestions of imagery in these *Instaglitches* belies their uncanniness. Apparently familiar imagery breaks down on closer, considered examination, revealing the contingency and imposed nature of their "*realist*" contents. Unlike historical abstractions which often attempted to achieve non-representational status,[55] these pictures aspire to be seen as representational, while clearly lacking any photographic basis. This nature separates *Instaglitch* imagery from the multitudinous products of "glitch" filters and other software which simulate familiar problems in digital images, such as macroblocking or compression errors that fragment and distort otherwise familiar imagery. These effects have proliferated online (and in the database of *Instagram*) as the clichés of Glitch Art which neither challenge interpretation nor attempt to cause any critical response from their audience; they are instances of the 'discursive aesthetic.'

The ambivalence of the *Instaglitch's* capacity to be recognized *as-glitched* creates a contingency limiting the 'discursive aesthetic' common to digital work by neither being readily identifiable as "error" nor being readily assimilable by other types of Glitch Art posed on the *Instagram* platform, yet

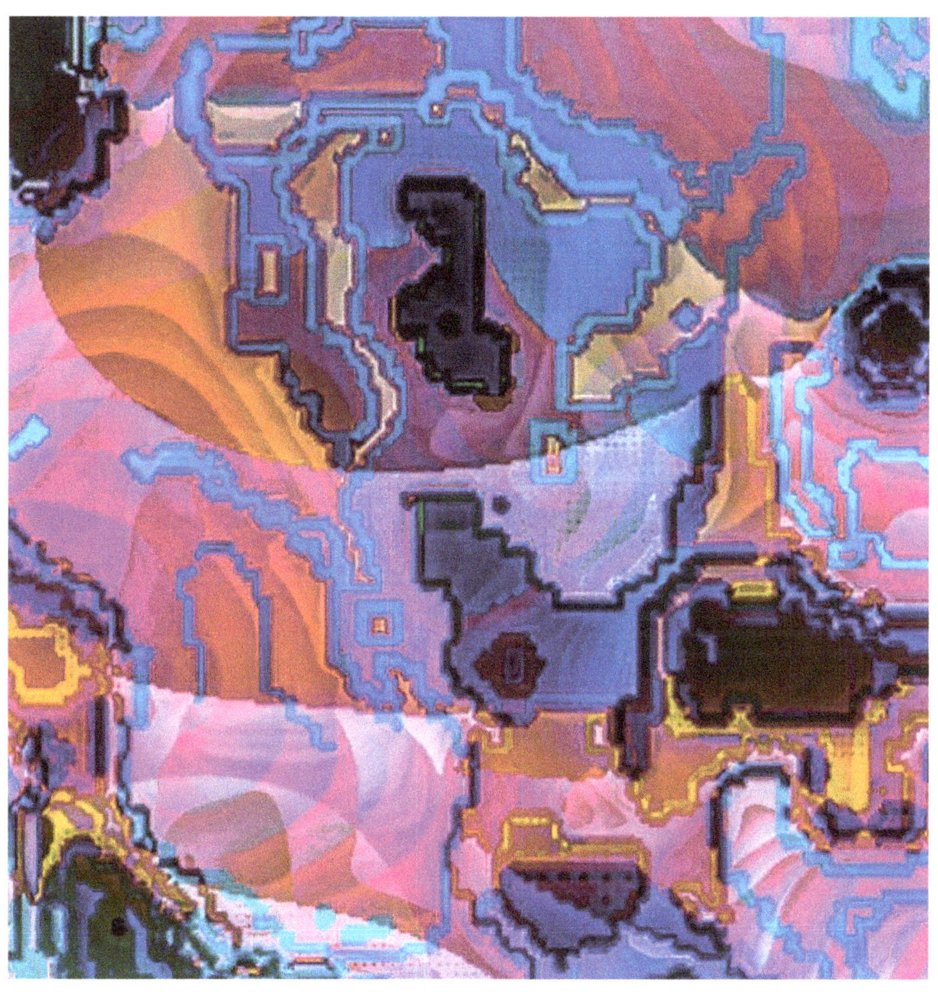

Figure 3.4: *Instaglitch_41476766_2209971759249345_4250947655254004 55_n*
copyright © 2018 Michael Betancourt
courtesy Artists Rights Society (ARS)

their origins with a "glitch" is not in doubt. These distinctions are essential: they allow these works to cue their construction—"made it with the Instagram app"—as a critical challenge to that app's normative operations. They continue my investigation and engagement with 'glitches as a visual medium' that informs my critico-theoretical critique of digital capitalism and its operations, challenging the normative dimensions of social media and its constraints on human use.

Instaglitches demonstrate that 'critical art' is not merely "raising consciousness" to addresses a set of given (reified) mechanisms of domination, but of fostering a self-referential, conscious engagement where the audience recognizes and acknowledges their role in maintaining the *status quo*—whatever it may be. The traditional, critical act of 'raising consciousness' is always concerned with bringing the audience to a specific *a priori* political action, one in which one mechanism of dominance is exchanged for another; instead, my critical works are not addressing any singular political change, (always proximate), but with fostering an actively engaged way of *being* in the world. The self-referentiality the *Instaglitches* offer the viewer is one without a specific political agenda, suggesting instead a mode of interpretation that begins with a self-consciousness about experience and how its *as-if* interpretation identifies the audience's internal constraints as the superficially externalized, normative instrumentalities of the *transparent mode.*

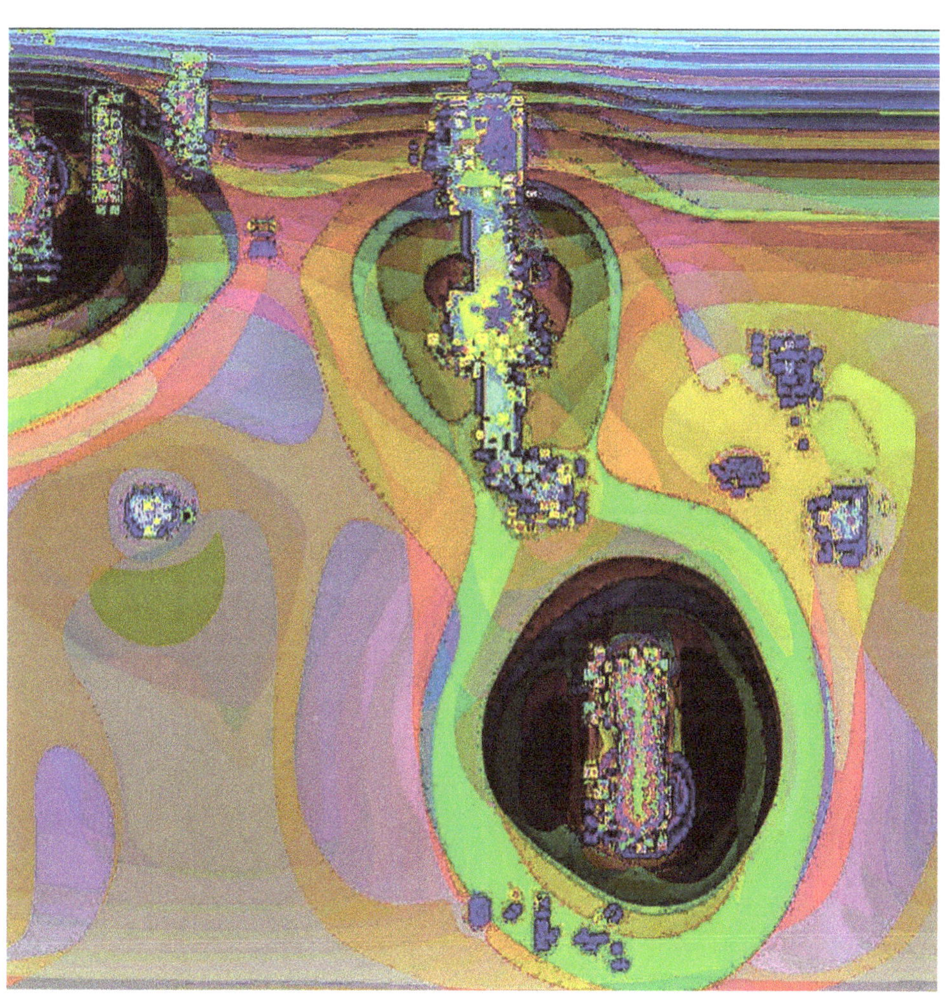

Figure 3.5: *Instaglitch_68675185_405686730081637_1401474340170901318_n*

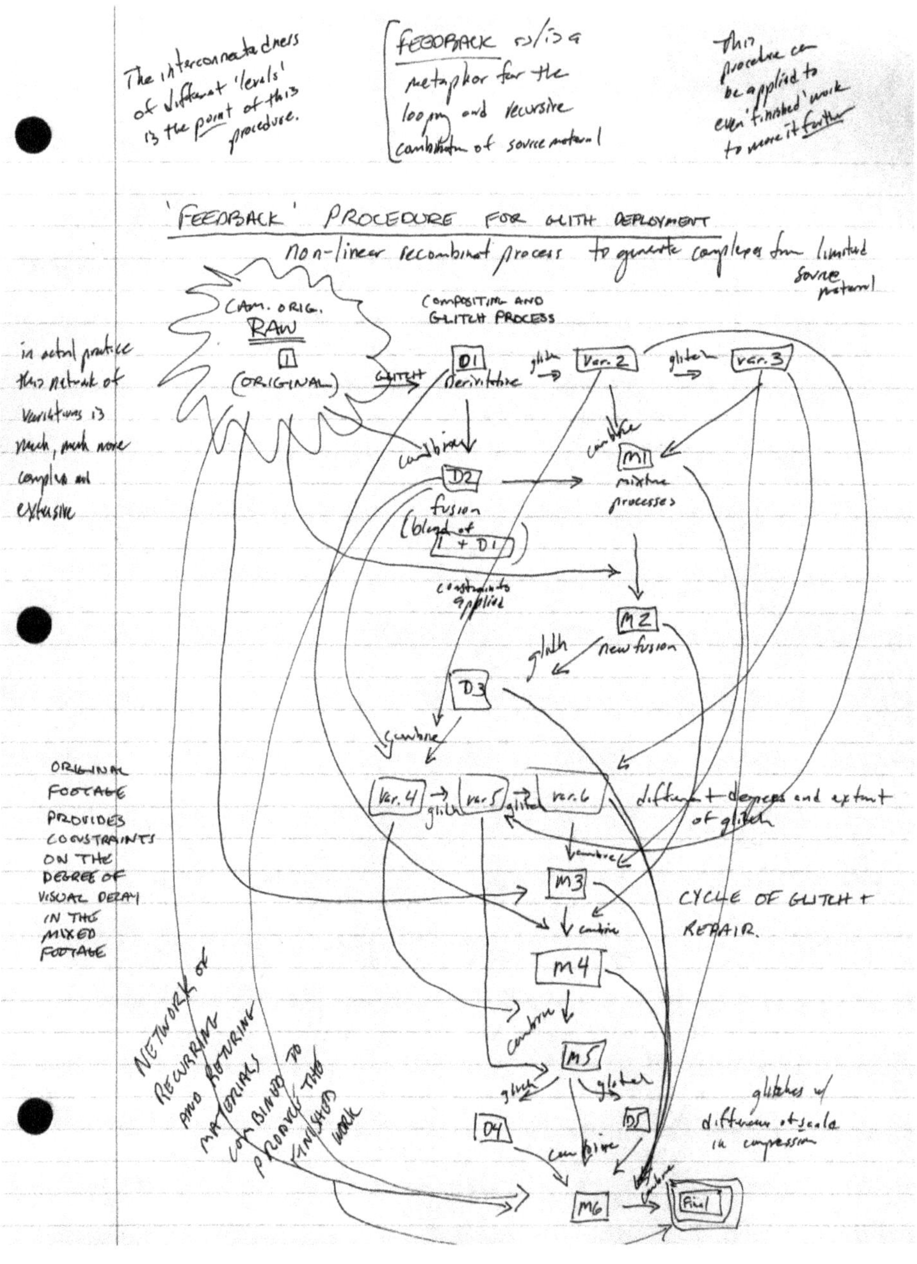

Figure 4.1: A recursive process of digital compositing and re-glitching applied to create "raw" footage for use in the finished movie.

4
Retrieval Errors

Archival films and videos provide a foundation for the processing used in all my glitch movies, including *Contact Light* (2012), *Dancing Glitch* (2013), *The Kodak Moment* (2013), *The Dark Rift* (2014), *The Dogs of Space* (2015) and the serial *Going Somewhere* (2016–2018). It functions as a mechanism to engage with familiar imagery and formal cinematic structure, while at the same time subverting that foundation through the fragmentation produced by databending and datamoshing. These techniques create interruptions and unexpected results in the rendering of the digitally encoded file that are entirely different from historical montage or editing.[56] My use of archival materials belongs to the lineage of appropriation and recombination that were common features of media art and artist's media throughout the twentieth century.[57] From the use of newspapers and other printed matter in Cubist and Dadaist collage to Soviet montage, archives are central to practices that use reproduced materials, repurposed and transformed. These methods have been a consistent dimension of archival reuse in cinema that is commonly called 'found footage,'[58] one that continues into the present with the disruptions and repetitions prominent in Glitch Art.

The specific role of digitized archival materials in my own movies brings these historical relationships between production, post-production, and digital re-composition into consciousness as inherent to media practice.[59] The quotational transformation of the archive via the remix attenuates the recognizable source through the material functions of digital artifacts and the visible presence of compression, ironically bringing the role of the archive into consciousness as a challenge to the originary identity of the source material. This dimension of familiarity is precisely the reason for the footage selected for use in my work; its arrangement as visual music substitutes for narrative structure.

The role of archival procedures is fundamental to the editing of motion pictures. Whether the images are created new, or taken from existing movies, the process of editing them into a finished work follows a singular protocol: all the shots to be edited are collected, sorted, and catalogued as part of the editorial selection, resulting in an archival record that is then mobilized into/as the *montage* which creates the production shown on-screen—a fact that allows not only a fixed order of shots, but their algorithmic reassembly based on user input. This instrumental use of archival procedures in movies presents a duality as not only an implicit aspect of all media production, but as a feature of 'found footage' cinema in particular. The appropriation process replaces the use of newly-created footage with that taken from archival sources: an already existing media work is sampled and then reassembled and/or combined with new materials into a production that is qualitatively different in meaning from its original source(s). Editorial selection is a generally neglected-but-essential transformative practice in discussions of archival materials that tend to focus instead on the *source* of material rather than the protocols of its dis/assembly into new works. Yet this dualism is precisely relevant to my uses of archival material in creating glitch movies: while the materials being assembled could be from anywhere, they follow the same archival and manipulation (glitch) protocols that serve to efface the assembly by *montage* from the finished work. Instead of juxtaposed shots, one image flows into the next, a continuous transformation without the interruptions posed by 'cuts.'

An Archival Paradox

The 2 minute movie *The Kodak Moment* uses two archival shots of the silent film actress Mae Murray contained in a Kodak test reel exposed at Paragon Studios in Fort Lee, New Jersey to demonstrate a new color film stock in 1921; they were chosen because this footage corresponds to the standard framing of a *medium shot* [MS] and a *close up* [CU], allowing for their sequencing to loop and repeat images, thus re-creating the familiar *découpage* of continuity editing from commercial narrative film. This (re)assembly masked the editing through established cinematic convention: as Murray turned towards, then away from the camera, these shots are cut together to produce an apparently seamless continuity of action familiar from commercial narrative cinema. Repetitions of shots and their digital transformation (flipping them horizontally, running them backwards) allowed the creation of a familiar seamless edited sequence. This editorial assembly enables a series of ruptures in framing and view which the audience can understand traditionally as a *realist* presentation, allowing her actions to appear as uninterrupted gestures while being fragmented via two distinct framings. The glitching process attacked and elided this conventional structure, producing something radically different in affect, undermining their articulation and fragmentation, resulting in a continuous shot (the datastream) that imitates the long take in its formal appearance, yet is paradoxically composed from two different framings [CU, MS] at the same time. The digital breakdown imposes an awareness of an uninterrupted datastream rather than paired, edited shots.

Glitch procedures create *unheimlich* archival footage: *mis*function dominates the finished movie by disassembling the edited sequence of archival shots and complicating their archival recognition. Clearly apparent visual "ruptures" shown by the 'material function' transform this edited sequence into an unquestionably *digital* product. The experience of the work is reflexive, drawing attention to its basis as a 'technical image': cueing attention to the immanent and immediate rendering of the image seen on-screen as an *encounter.* It shows the digital capacity to alter, blend, and reconfigure 'found footage' into a new singular "shot"[60] whose identity as a coherent unit is unstable. One shot does not end so the next can begin in *The Kodak Moment*—the precise boundaries that mark a 'cut' in film are absent from the datastream's continuous articulation, bringing the constancy of the digital to attention as a variant on the 'long take' without making any ontological claims about the reality of its subject matter or the factuality of its production. The glitch procedures dominate the finished movie to such an extent that the source footage effectively vanishes into the procedural order, but without losing its identity as *archival*.

Cinema modulates experience via technology: the presentation of the datastream as a found artifact emerges from the familiar techniques of datamoshing, in which a video compressed using the MPEG-1/MPEG-2 specification [where the video frames are divided into frames with image data (I-frames) and frames with motion data (p-frames)] is altered to eliminate the image data (I-frames), resulting in characteristic streaks, flows, and fragmentation,[61] a process that media historian Gregory Zinman explains:

> Datamoshing involves the removal of an encoded video's I-frames ("intra-coded picture," also known as key frames—a frame that does not require any information regarding another frame to be decoded), leaving only the P- ("predicted picture") or B- ("bi-predictive picture") frames. P-frames contain information predicting the change sin the image between the current frame and the previous one, and B-frames contain information predicting the image differences between the previous, current and subsequent frames. Because P- and B-frames use data from previous and forward frames, they are more compressed than I-Frames.[62]

These impacts are predictable, highly dramatic, and seemingly autonomous: this procedure eliminates the high resolution image data, preventing the periodic 'refresh' that differentiates one shot from another. It creates a continuous flow from one frame into the next, ignoring any existing editing. Because datamoshing dedifferentiates shots, it allows databending using a hexadecimal editor to propagate the changed values in the data file itself without being 'corrected.' These are integral changes, foundational alterations, that do more than just cause one shot to flow into the next: they alter the values of the data being displayed.[63] Changing the data in a digital file—replacing all values such as "AF" with "AE"—creates permanent alterations

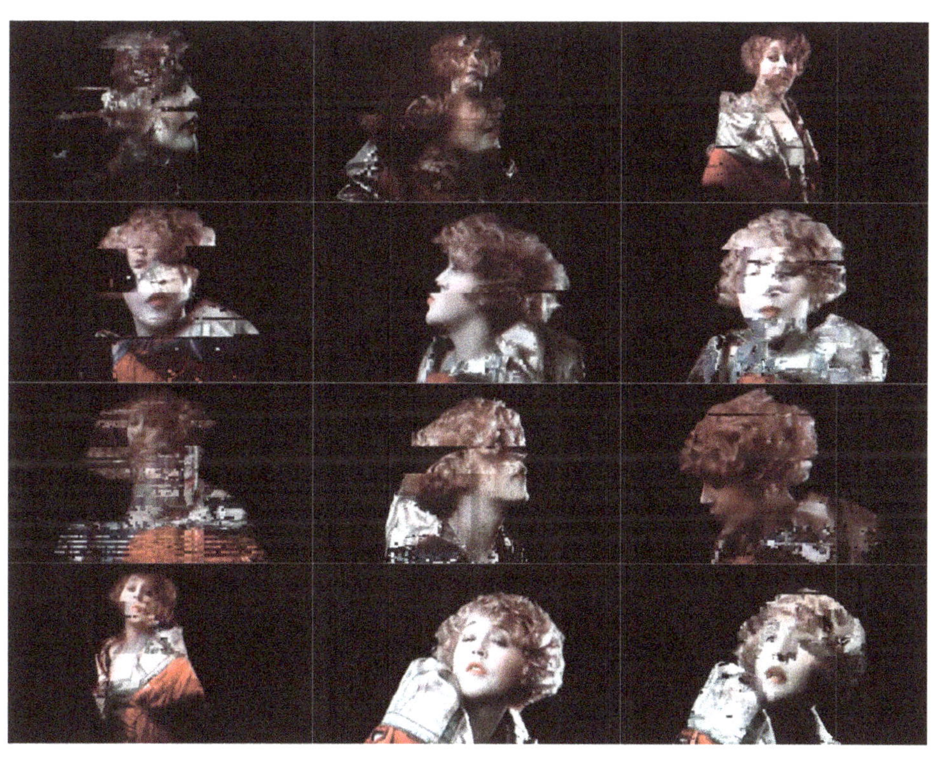

Figure 4.2: Stills from *The Kodak Moment*
copyright © 2013 Michael Betancourt
courtesy Artists Rights Society (ARS)

in the rendering of that data by the digital computer. These distortions and other breakdowns are especially pronounced with compressed data. This process of material editing and revision results in purely determinate results; for a given set of compression settings, the changes can be anticipated with practice—much like playing an instrument without stops—giving a high degree of control over the kinds of glitches and distortions thus generated. *The Kodak Moment* uses a recursive process of digital compositing [Figure 4.1] to fuse both the edited archival footage and the glitched variations created through datamoshing and databending into a new result, the finished movie. The characteristic banding and fragmentation familiar from glitched videos overlies the equally familiar continuity edit of Mae Murray's actions, but with an essential difference: there is no editing between shots even though the framework of that earlier edit is still present.

The results of this compositing, processing, and editorial arrangement is both and neither archival nor newly created: the *generative* potentials of my digital approach to archival material differ from those of analogue media both procedurally and qualitatively, even though they derive from the now-historical processes of optical printing[64] and video synthesis.[65] Understanding it in terms of its differences and convergences with "found film" is instructive in considering the role of archival materials in this digital transformation/combination of old and new. The use of these two distinct views of Mae Murray in *The Kodak Moment* undermines traditional continuity cutting because the glitch process replaces the edited shots with shifting bands allowing both [CU] and [MS] to appear simultaneously. They interpenetrate, and the glitch elides the 'jumps' created by cutting to show the imagery as moving, overlapping, and pseudo-independent "bands." Not simply superimposed, each "change-in-shot" emerges from a shifting composition of image-blocks against a black background. What are distinct camera positions/shots in the original 'found footage' disappear into a continuous progression without the distinctions created by cutting, but it still retains the distinct identity of each 'shot.'

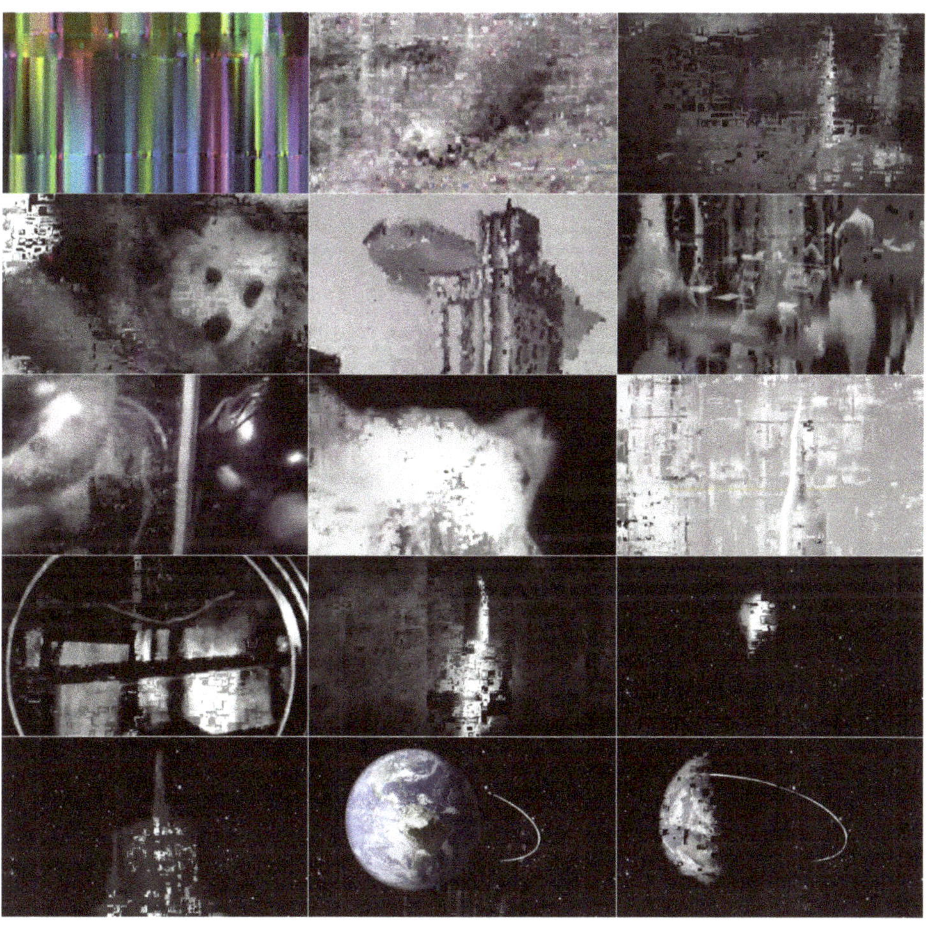

Figure 4.3: Stills from *The Dogs of Space*
copyright © 2015 Michael Betancourt
courtesy Artists Rights Society (ARS)

The 'material function' announces the formative basis of these images as an immanent product of digital processing, a recognition that challenges the *historical* assertions of archival footage—a collapse of time and history into immanence. This attenuation of archival sources makes that quotational basis evident as a paradox of recognitions and displacements between the original footage and the identification of these images as sampled data, thus drawing attention to the contingency of media. Every movie depends on the particular construction of the technology itself for its existence. Critically, this capacity depends on the audience recognizing that what they see is a product of a technical artifice—apparent in the 'material function' of the glitches, but implicit in all media—that demonstrates the assumed recognition of the archival footage is a fallacy. The invocation of past knowledge and expertise revealed by this digital metamorphosis of sources is also an revelation that the imposition of such recognitions creates a new and different set of conditions for the organization and presentation of the materials seen on-screen, one that derives from the nostalgic reverie enabled as/by the archival identification in itself. This discovery is the self-conscious interplay between these decomposed shots and their familiar understanding as representational imagery—the identification of the woman, Mae Murray, and her actions that tease the camera/audience.

Digital Metamorphosis

Digitization imposes an essential difference between an original analogue source and its digital doppelgänger. Each glitch in movies such as *Contact Light* (2012) or *The Kodak Moment* demonstrates that historical 'found footage' taken from archival films is limited in ways that computational media are not: filmed shots are fixed compositions that offer only a limited degree of transformation without the re-productive intervention of optical printing or the material assault on the film base itself. Historian Jonathan Walley notes how this difference between analogue and digital technologies challenge the continuity between earlier

Digital glitches reveal a 'material function' for media that determines their identification and prescribes their semantics on-screen. These complex problematics of immanence and invisibility define the technical failure or "glitch" as a relational designation (neither "signal" nor "noise") that bounds their critical and expressive potentials. The dynamic focus of my work emerges through visual semiosis via the ambiguities and complexities of this tension between expectation and encounter that offers these critically-oriented misfunctions as an aesthetic engagement with the realist ideology of digital mediation, recognizable as an opposition of recognition and reality.

media and contemporary digital work, especially apparent in the role of archival materials:

> The key to understanding these works is their preoccupation with the *difficulties* that the film medium presents: its clunky mechanical nature and resistance to ease of use. Also emphasized is the complex, component nature of film: the multiple chemical, mechanical and optical components and operations that require mastery, and the possibility of glitches inherent in each one.[66]

The technical failures of the obsolescent celluloid cinema creates very different technical failures and errors than digital technology, apparent in how the 'shot' is an inherent feature of film, and its continued relevance for digital media reflects the assumption that the images and shots displaced on-screen are stable, discrete units—precisely the distinction that datamoshing challenges [Figure 4.4]. The decoding process gives digital movies an aura of information, but the prescriptive language of digital technology is error-prone—it exhibits a sensitive dependence on the particulars of the file (a factor that increases dramatically with compressed data). Both the particular shots and the individual frames that form them—is a constant, even axiomatic, belief about motion pictures that makes the archival reuse of 'found footage' a fundamental potential of cinema generally. Digital glitches show these shots are procedurally

Figure 4.4 [following pages]: The manipulation of footage by *datamoshing* (and the problems it makes for editing).

EXPLOITS IN THE LAND OF **OBSOLETE** VIDEO COMPRESSION: **MPEG-1 & MPEG-2**

TIME MANAGEMENT PROTOCOL

DATAMOSHING CONVERTS A VIDEO INTO A CONTINUOUS STREAM OF MOTION TRANSFORMATIONS WITHOUT BEING "CORRECTED."

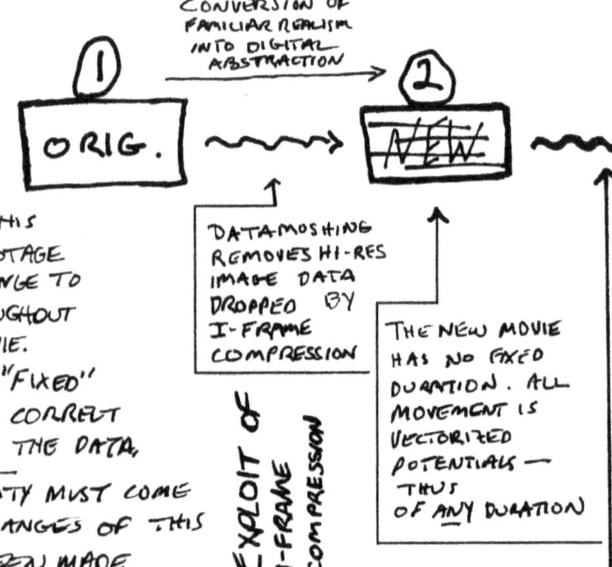

DATABENDING THIS DATAMOSHED FOOTAGE ALLOWS ANY CHANGE TO CONTINUE THROUGHOUT THE ENTIRE MOVIE. OTHERWISE IT IS "FIXED" WHEN I-FRAMES CORRECT FOR ERRORS IN THE DATA.

FIXING FOR PARITY MUST COME AFTER ANY CHANGES OF THIS TYPE HAVE BEEN MADE.

PARITY

CORRECT FOR MISSED FRAMES TO MAINTAIN AUDIO-VISUAL SYNC

ORIG ①

M A T C H

GLITCH ②

FRAMES LOST MUST BE RECALCULATED

DATAMOSHING INVOLVES REMOVING FRAMES FROM THE ORIGINAL FOOTAGE ①. THE NEW MOVIE MUST BE SPEEDRAMPED BACK TO THE DURATION OF ORIGINAL ON A SHOT-BY-SHOT BASIS TO RETURN TO SYNC. THESE CHANGES GIVE THE NEW MOVIE AN UNCANNY INSTABILITY AS SHOTS FLOW TOGETHER BUT THEIR AUDIBLE CUES REMAIN CONSTANT.

THESE INSTABILITIES DESTABILIZE SYNC CREATING A MISSED CONNECTION BY DRAWING ATTENTION TO ITS ARBITRARY NATURE — SYNC AS IMPOSED.

RECOMBINATIONS

+ ORIG

+ GLITCH

+ PROCESS

TIME CORRECTIONS TO MATCH ① ALLOWS FOR MIXTURES AND RECOMBINATIONS OF ③ WITH OTHER FOOTAGE AND PROCEDURES TO MAKE MORE COMPLEX HYBRIDS.

③ T.S.

TIME STRETCHED

VARIATIONS OF FOOTAGE

A

B

C

(ETC.)

MATERIAL TO EDIT & COMPOSITE INTO FINAL MOVIE.

THIS PROCESS CAN BE PERFORMED RECURSIVELY: TO EDIT THIS MATERIAL REQUIRES IT BE STABILIZED [NORMALIZED] WHICH RESTORES THE VIDEO TO A STANDARD ENCODING, BUT WITH NEW I-FRAMES.

IMAGE DATA (I-FRAMES) CREATE THE APPEARANCE OF FAMILIAR REALITY. REMOVING THEM GIVES THE RESULT A NEW, DIGITAL CONNECTION — BUT ALSO MISCONNECTS THE RESULTING VIDEO TO 'THE REAL'. THE DIGITAL MEDIUM SUBSTITUTES FOR THE OTHER LINK TO REALITY, OFFERING ITSELF AS REAL INSTEAD.

MISSING ONE CONNECTION MEANS MAKING ANOTHER. FOOTAGE EITHER SUGGESTS A TELEOLOGICAL CONNECTION TO 'THE REAL' OR IT CONNECTS TO SOMETHING ELSE. GLITCHED FOOTAGE REPLACES 'THE REAL' WITH ITS OWN ENCODING, BUT ASSERTS THE "REALITY" OF THE MEDIUM, THAT THE ENCODING IS REAL, WHICH MAKES THE UNCANNY MAINTANCE OF SYNC HAPPEN — THE ERROR AS NOT-ERROR.

REALISM FINDS A WAY TO RETURN AS THE REALITY OF THE MEDIUM

MISMATCHES OF EXPECTATION AND ENCOUNTER — THE MISSED CONNECTION OF REALITY AND IMAGE — IS AMBIVALENT. THIS INSTABILITY IS THE END-GOAL OF THIS PROTOCOL FOR USING AND MANAGING DATAMOSHED VIDEO.

generated, a foundational difference exceeding earlier methods of archival reuse in 'found footage.' Where the range of films repurposing shots from earlier films [that includes avant-garde films such as Joseph Cornell's *Rose Hobart* (1936), or Bruce Conner's *A Movie* (1958), or Bill Morrison's *Decasia* (2002)] is considerable, they remain within the limitations of what their shots *are*: the reassembly process does not reconfigure the fundamental contents of the shots in themselves. The assembly protocol for 'found footage' used these films differs only in the imagery employed; they are works of cinematic montage. They rearrange existing shots to create a new motion picture that is indexically connected to the originary sources in other films, even as their significance departs from these historical sources. The recognition of these quotation-extracts is part of their new use, marking the similarity of this '*archival function*' in both film as well as in the meme or remix.[67] The distinctions in these uses fall within a range based on the degree of recognition—as being from a specific source, or more generally as "quotational." In those cases where the identification of source is central to the new meaning, as in some memes or in Cornell's *Rose Hobart*, this identification is what Eco termed the "postmodern aesthetic solution" to intertextuality—where the identification is central to the significance:

> What is more interesting is when the quotation is explicit and recognizable, as happens in post modern literature and art, which blatantly and ironically play on the intertextuality ... aware of the quotation, the spectator is brought to elaborate ironically on the nature of such a device and to acknowledge the fact that one has been invited to play upon one's encyclopedic knowledge.[68]

This recognition of source is not only an allusive "*I've seen that before!*" that comes from familiarity, but is also an identification of transformation—that what appears is not entirely the same as the original. However, even when the sources for individual shots do not necessarily become apparent as an intertextual dialogue between the immanent use and the identified source, the archive

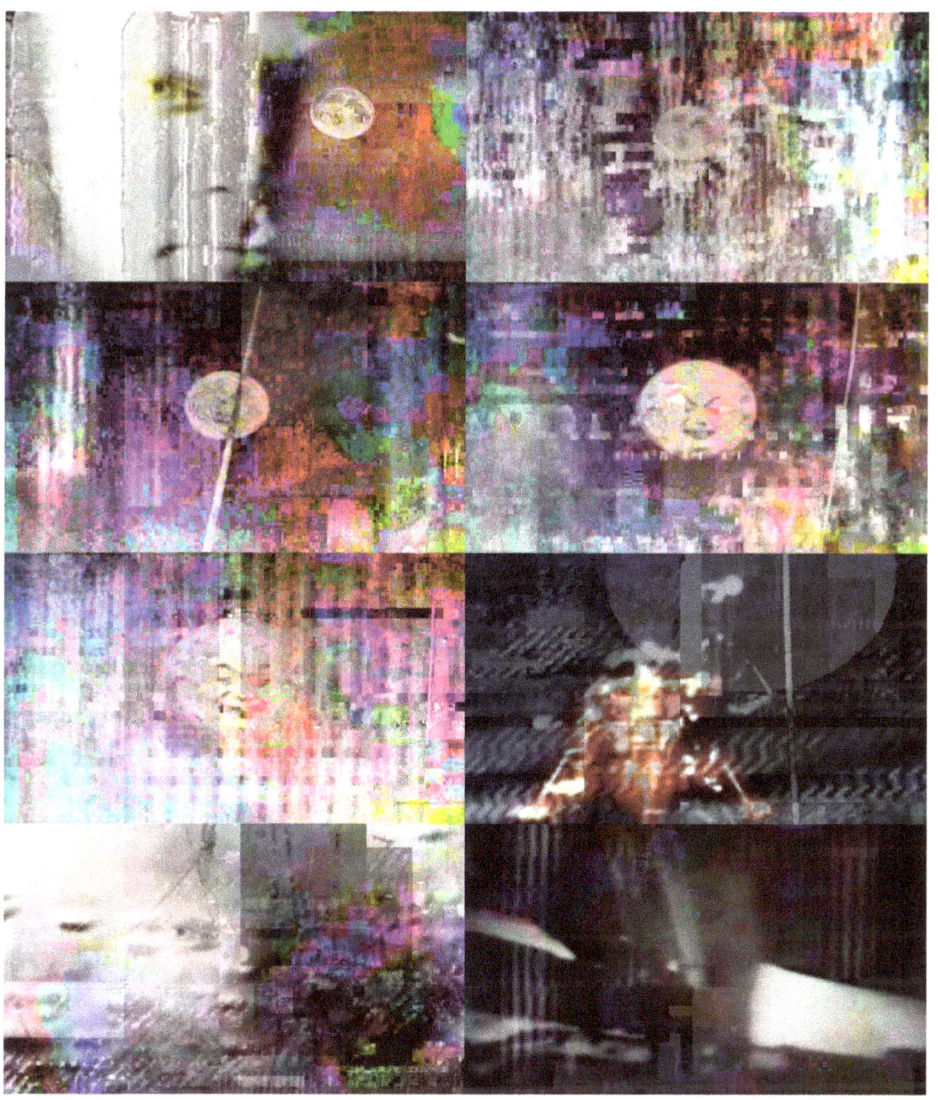

Figure 4.5: Stills from *Contact Light* copyright © 2012 Michael Betancourt courtesy Artists Rights Society (ARS)

is immanent in this historical 'found footage' precisely because it cannot be avoided: Cornell's film is concerned with *who* appears in the shots, not *where* the shots came from; Conner's film draws from both fiction and non-fiction (newsreels and documentaries) equally; Morrison's damaged and decaying film is as much a documentary presentation of lost films as it is a montage sequence concerned with entropy and social breakdowns. In all these cases, the shots remain constants: their form and framing do not change. The designation of an archival source creates the recognition that the work is a variation on an established order; intertextuality invokes a connection to an absent original. It valorizes the archive. The "encyclopedic knowledge" that is central to Eco's proposal informs *The Kodak Moment* on the immanent level that articulates the encounter (continuity editing, the familiar relationship between one shot and the next that create an illusion of uninterrupted action across the cut) and on the mnemonic level that identifies the woman posing on-screen, Mae Murray. But both are attenuated. This recognition about the digital image informs the movies I make: *apparent motion* originates in the audience's cognitive engagement with multiple, fragmentary views of figures/spaces that become recognizable and unitary figures *experienced* as coherent-in-motion, even through when viewed as stills these 'frames' often do *not* contain or present single coherent figures but clearly fragmentary and incomplete parts juxtaposed in a disorderly fashion. These recognitions of contingency complicate and subvert the archival identification, as well as the sequential ordering of shots, and the role of cinematic realism this familiar organization invokes, cueing the viewer critically, and encouraging a critical response.

My movie *The Dogs of Space* (2015) demonstrates the "encyclopedic knowledge" Eco desrcibes. It uses shots of the 'space gun' at the conclusion of the 1936 science fiction film *Things to Come*, documentary footage of NASA Gemini launches from 1963, and newsreel shots of the "first space pop stars,"[69] Soviet space dogs Belka and Strelka, preparing for their launch on August 19, 1960. This 3 minute rhythmic montage

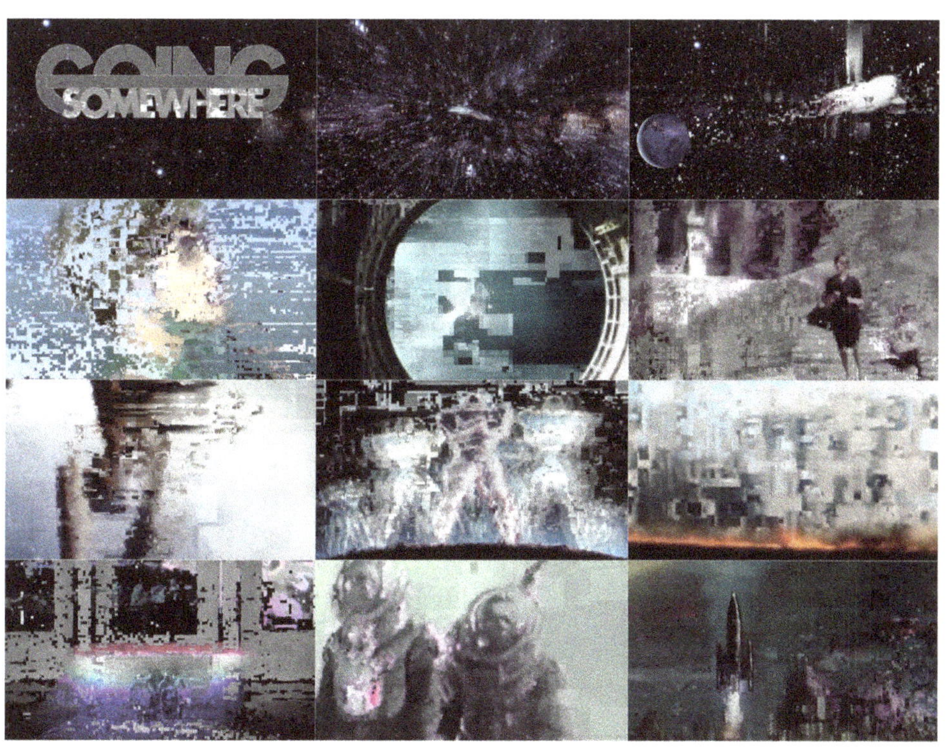

Figure 4.6: Stills from *Going Somewhere*
copyright © 2015–2018 Michael Betancourt
courtesy Artists Rights Society (ARS)

was synchronized with a musical remix made from the fanfares in Italian composer Ottorino Respighi's *The Fountains of Rome*. These archival materials were edited into a paranarrative with minimal reframing to accommodate the 16:9 aspect ratio of digital video. Glitches created new a new movie where the distinction between fiction and non-fiction breaks down, leaving only the digital artifact in its place. It is a reconfiguration of existing material that balances the recognitions of subject matter and archival sourcing with the interventions made possible by the change in medium.

Archival materials have a specific valence that is directly connected to their potential for instrumentality when reorganized. This semantic relationship of immanent use and intertextual recognition is an historical constant: whether it is seen as a record of past achievements to challenge (Modernist avant-garde) or contribute to (academic), a body of existing materials awaiting reassembly (Post-Modern anti-authorialism), the archive exists as a material reference point for studio praxis. The archives thus deployed are not merely metaphoric. Their sudden recognition is matched by an equally powerful realization that brings the historical, original source into the identification process: past experience becomes an immanent mediator of how the new work is being understood, a change in articulation matched by the shift from being a novel production to relying on the recognized connection to historical material that is essential to Eco's proposal.

Considering the *datastream* (information contained by/in the digital file) [Figure 4.7] as the fundamental material for digital art makes the emergence of 'Glitch Art' inevitable.[70] Datamoshing removes the "image" from the compressed datastream in the video file, leaving only the data about the motion vectors and their transformation over time: in place of carefully resolved images, what appears instead is a "echo" of the data that has been erased. Encoding motion as a separate element than the visuality of the pixels themselves enables a new kind of moving image, one that allows experimentation with movement in itself. There are suggestions of what the 'original' imagery was, but

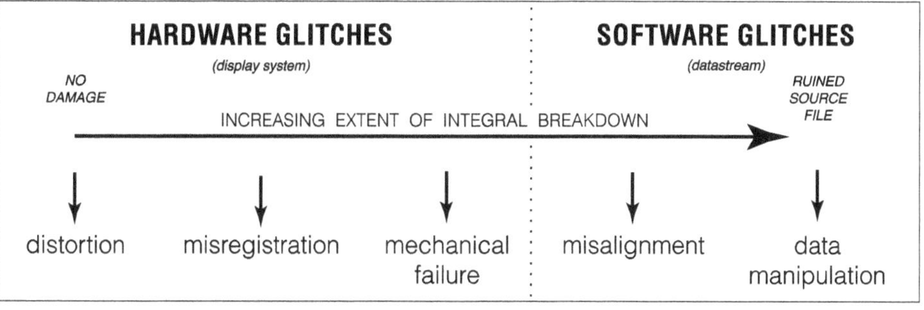

Figure 4.7: Empirical sources of the 'material function' created by various types of glitches in motion pictures.

datamoshing eliminates the fine 'photographic' details.[71] The results of that division between image and movement renders these glitched movies as potentially without a specific resolution or duration, able to extend the shots in duration and expand them in scale, thus exposing the articulation of generative media as a cognitive response by the audience.

The glitched materials in *The Dogs of Space* dominate the movie's appearance on-screen even more than they do in *The Kodak Moment*, simultaneously creating a new set of visuals resembling and derived from the archival sources, yet distinct from them. These transformations are all possible because digital media are an encoded datastream, a fact that gives their articulation an entirely different valence than the fixity of shots. This instability is what makes it of interest: the glitch procedures employed in this movie recreate the data corruption of incompletely downloaded, damaged files by both altering the data itself (*databending*) so that it converts into pixilated blocks, and selectively removing portions of the compressed datastream (datamoshing) so that the video smears and flows across the screen. These twin methods attenuate the familiarity of the archival materials without destroying their quotational recognition *as-archival*, nor erasing the identity of the shots employed. The Soviet space dogs Belka and Strelka are immediately recognizable, as are the familiar archival shots from the NASA Gemini mission, and the 'launch complex' and 'space gun' from *Things to Come*. The ability to identify the contents of these shots is countered by their visible abstraction. The resulting movie draws attention to the 'material function' of the glitch in a demonstration of the digital medium.

The contemporary emergence of digital re/production technologies has brought about a revitalization of the archive as a realm of recombination and appropriation where the already-made undergoes a quotational transformation that is qualitatively different than the collage and assemblage that is more familiar from historical, analogue media. These developments become obvious in the transformative capacities of digital technology to alter, rearrange, and generate entirely new productions which are nevertheless entirely subservient to their historical sources, offering a new relevance for archival materials in the apprehension of "novel" media productions. These new potentials become obvious in the differences between media art based on archival footage subjected to reassembly (the 'found footage' work) and those employing generative footage where the shots employ 'found objects,' but the shots are rendered entirely new for the productions that employ them, as in the use of video games to create machinima.[72]

Transformation and Appropriation

Although *all* digital media are technically generated on-demand at the moment of their reception, the absolute separation between the rote generation of a media file such as an MPEG-encoded video or MP3-encoded audio recording that always follows a prescribed path, or the dynamically interactive generation of a video game where a specified collection of materials are produced in response to audience demands, or the programmed generation by software such as Autodesk's *Maya* or Maxon's *Cinema4D* that allows the construction of materials to-be-rendered, and the generative processes of AI and algorithmic systems makes the range of computational generative action

Databending Protocol

[**1**] Open the file in a hexdecimal editing program.

[**2**] Open the find/replace dialogue.

[**3**] Use the "replace all" option to make a global search and replace to change values such as D3 to E3.

[**4**] Record the change and make note of the result.

[**5**] "Save as" a file with a new name.

Different viewing programs will render the databent file differently. Test the results using different programs. When the file can't be recompressed, but will play, use screen capture to save those results.

Tracking both compression codec/settings and changes made allows the identification and reuse of transformations, giving a high degree of control over the resulting glitches.

apparent. The identification of *digital media* made through its material appearance as being-digital—most commonly through glitches—is an understanding of these media as empirical signs, as *things-in-themselves* that lack other meaning than their own identity as the result of digital technology. This identification arises from the audience's fluency with engaging 'technical images' and demonstrates their capacity to apply that knowledge to their immanent encounter.

Archival material can enter into this generative process at any point, or every point, informing and constraining what results. These limits on action are potentially a literal re/use of archival material as well as simultaneously being a conceptual mapping that establishes the essential expectations for signification. Without an established wealth of past experience, fluency, and expertise, meaning becomes impossible; audiences thus bring the archive with them to all their encounters, using it to inform their particular encounters, making this aspect of its role at once omnipresent and banal. The historical assertion of this indexicality for media work as a critical challenge to originality and uniqueness are well known.

The circulation and recirculation of digital images and movies via appropriations such as remix depend on a *transparent* archival recognition that is categorically different than the role of familiar identification in either 'found footage' films, or the use of stock footage in both narrative fiction or documentary media. My seven minute series of movie serials, *Going Somewhere* (2016–2018), explores these potentials throughout all six episodes via a quotational attenuation of sources. The selection process emphasized iconic imagery in footage taken from a range of historical sources in both popular culture and NASA archives [Figure 4.6], while the soundtrack is a musical remix of minor themes from Gustav Holst's suite *The Planets*, juxtaposed to evoke familiar science fiction scores that borrow themes from this composition, such as John William's score for *Star Wars* (1977). The same protocols of editorial reassembly and glitching employed in *The Kodak Moment* and *The Dogs of Space* were used to alter and recombine footage for this serial movie;

however, instead of simply accepting the framing provided in the source footage as in *The Kodak Moment*, the partial reconstruction performed in *The Dogs of Space* was the model for these movies. In all the serial episodes of *Going Somewhere* every shot was digitally recomposed, retouched, and often the visual effects were rebuilt prior to being glitched—even before the datamoshing and databending procedurally reorganized their contents. *Adobe AfterEffects* was used to produce the finished composites of glitched and non-glitched archival material. The scope of materials used was not limited to only *moving images*—historical photographs, graphics, and texts—throughout the series ASCii text versions of the unglitched original edited video were composited along with the glitched video as a mechanism of drawing attention to the concept of digital and narrative encoding. This wide variety of materials all show the science fiction iconography of robots, space ships, visiting the Moon, and journeying to alien worlds. Their selection and arrangement conforms to the familiar narrative schemas of familiar sci-fi movies, without employing footage from those movies in the new work.

The elemental recognition identified by Eco is attenuated in these archival manipulations of existing materials, rendered obvious through the process of being digitally 'broken' by the glitch techniques of databending and datamoshing. The 'material function' of the glitch[73] makes the familiar 'transparent' engagement with media into a self conscious feature of the movie, making the connections between the image's apparent indexicality, cinematic realism, and the encultured role of past experience in the identification of "noise" obvious as the technical failure (glitch) is never "only" a technical failure: it also always *signifies* "technical failure." These dynamics of recognition and rejection are central to philosopher Jacques Attali's comments about the distinction of *music* from *noise* as the central factor for coherent interpretation:

> With noise is born disorder and its opposite: the world.
> With music is born power and its opposite: subversion.

> In noise can be read the codes of life, the relations among them. Clamor, Melody, Dissonance, Harmony; when it is fashioned by man with specific tools, when it invades man's time, when it becomes sound, noise is the source of purpose and power, of the dream—music.[74]

Attali's observation that "noise" separates the ambiguous and unknown play of things into significance and insignificance—those factors that the material role of a glitch specifically undermines and troubles by making the "noise" into a signifier in/of itself. This transformation fragments the archival imagery into its constituent pixels: the motion shown on-screen becoming a metastable field of continuous change. In place of familiar images is the continuous series of changes made visible by datamoshing, and then highlighted by databending—and the errors/distortions they produce: as with *The Kodak Moment* and *Dogs of Space*, these glitch processes eliminate the editing of shots in *Going Somewhere*. Yet the original source materials remain recognizable in spite of these transformations. The archive is always immanent in glitched movies as both a source for the materials and their 'degree zero'—the indexicality of the shots is not to a profilmic reality, but to the archival footage that undergoes transformation. This connection to the archive brings its instrumentalization into focus as a matrix of materials that are subject to interrogation, deflection, quotation, substitution—all the formal manipulations familiar from language and its articulations within a limited matrix of pre-extant terms. 'Found footage' transformed in these ways offers an immanent demonstration of the parallels between digital protocols of image presentation/retrieval and those of lexical expertise, suggesting that these archival operations share the same foundation in past experience as all semiotic constructions, textual or visual.

In addressing the role of archival materials in my glitch movies what matters about their construction is not the use of the materiality of digital media, but the ways that materiality becomes a vehicle for interrupting and altering the relationships to their familiar basis in the archive. This reworking of historical material, as well as the familiar tropes of cinematic articulation, narrative, and aesthetics reveals the intertextual basis for the identifications of archival sources is the same as the other kinds of identification that render media coherent. The transposition of cinematic techniques developed for photographic motion pictures shown on celluloid to the ethereal and immaterial order created by a digital signal demonstrates how established expertise is essential to any recognition connected to these kinetic media. The utility of archival materials as a demonstration of this discursive aesthetic engagement is self-evident. They are a mechanism that acknowledges history and tradition through the morphology and structure of imagery that parallels the role of digital manipulations that draw attention to the materiality of the digital as a medium, thus highlighting the temporal relationships evident in the act of watching, the transformations being shown, and the archival origins of that material in still other productions—a recursive directing of attention to the *time* of its encounter/presentation on-screen.

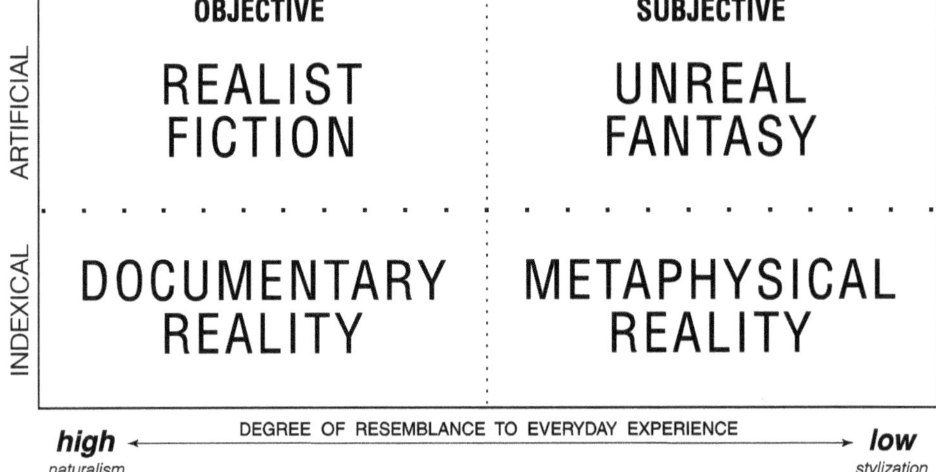

Figure 5.1: The four realist modes are defined by the relationships between *naturalism::stylization* and *indexicality::artificiality.* These oppositions distinguish "objective" and "subjective" via audience expectations: when matched with an indexical claim is understood to describe some aspect of 'the real,' while an artificial claim (as in abstract photography) identifies instead an entirely unreal presentation.

5
Realist Fallacy

Those things everyone knows about photography makes talking about *abstraction* seem utterly pointless—the most self-evident element of photography is also is its most commonly unconsidered: it is "the medium of absolute realism."[75] Because we find its *naturalism* to be a completely self-evident quality it leaves us with the feeling that *of course* photography is *realist* in depiction, as critic Susan Sontag explicitly states: "Photography furnishes evidence. Something we hear about, but doubt, seems proven when we're shown a photograph of it."[76] This belief is the problem photographer Jeff Wall described:

> Photography's own historical evolution into Modernist discourse has been determined by the fact that, unlike the older arts, it cannot dispense with depiction and so, apparently cannot participate in the adventure it might be said to have suggested in the first place.[77]

Conceiving photography as being irreducibly representational (*naturalistic*) allows these claims to be made with impunity. However, *realism* in photography is a cultural construct, ratified by art world traditions and mundane belief,[78] that is at least partially held in place by critics of photography.[79] An "abstract photograph"? Such a thing is either impossible or absurd, an attempt to cover-up for technical failings, poor optical focus, incompetence. Hripsime Visser, the curator of photography at the Stedelijk Museum Amsterdam, explains these unquestioned assumptions about the nature of the photographic:

> The central problem for photography—and I am not the first one to point this out—is content, pure and simple. A photograph is first and foremost about something. There are those photography lovers who take this fundamental

> truth so much to heart that they consider more transparent forms of photography, like documentary and journalistic reportage, as the only true ones; the rest is considered propaganda, as in the case of fashion and advertising photography, or art.[80]

Stylization is allowed, but to a minimal degree and no more. *Realism* derives from the *transparent mode's* resemblance between the depiction and its viewer's everyday experiences—the assumed 'essential nature' of photography [Figure 5.1]. However, the insistence on "transparency" that characterizes the "photography lovers" is not a requirement for being a photograph, even though Wall implies that many people who are involved feel that it should be. He denies the range of other potentials developing around *stylization* by allowing only the *naturalistic* depiction to have any role in understanding photography.

Any "abstract-seeming" photograph is, according to this conception, actually only an isolation of something real, a clandestine *realism*. Thus, a photograph cannot be abstract, because then it would cease to be a photograph: those traces left by light passing through the optics of a camera that form an image. Think of photo-ids, the photo-finish, and a photographic memory. All present us with an essential tie to reality through their depiction. This is why we say of a photograph that it *is* what it shows, a diagnostic. These restrictions imposed on photography by its historical *naturalism* are restrictions that abstract photography pioneer, the photographer Franz Roh, recognized in 1964:

> Likenesses, actual landscapes and original reportage are, [the opponents of abstract photography] allege, the sole themes with which a photograph ought to concern itself. As soon as it becomes "non-representational," like modern painting or graphic art, it is straying along an alien path, degenerating into mere imitation of another form or art and simultaneously losing the real charms of its special technique.[81]

The restriction to *only* those images created as an ontological trace left by the passage of light through optics seems reasonable and poses a definition for photographs that intuitively feels right, until we begin looking at the marginalia it creates: what about "pin hole" photography, where there are no optics, only a minute hole poked in a piece of foil or cardboard? These images have a degree of focus, are immediately recognizable as photographs, yet they are made without the benefit of a lens—there are no actual *optics* involved—yet the results remain as photographs, however fuzzy and out-of-focus the result may be. But if the need for optics is purely optional,[82] then the assumption of the *realism* those optics so often produce is also open to question, and the "abstract photograph" returns quite insistently as something requiring consideration.

At the same time, other limits and exclusions, such as the demand for specific photo-chemical emulsions and darkroom processing would necessarily exclude all forms of electronic imaging, something that does not feel right when considering how people speak of their cellphone camera and it's images—as *photographs*. To restrict photography to only chemical processes—the photosensitive salts that respond to light and create the traditional photography of the darkroom—also means that all those images involving electronics cannot be photographs: not just the digital image, but the whole history of video and television as well; this denial is absurd. Photography no longer requires chemical traces, yet we still treat these electronic images as belonging to the same realm as the silver halide image. Without this limitation, the prospect of abstraction in photography not only seems plausible, but unavoidable. The artificial and fluid manipulation of electronic imaging has always been closer to the abstract than to *realism*, but only because it is so much more difficult to manipulate and plastically deform the silver halide image than images made from pixels. But the difficulty of manipulation and abstraction is not the same as its impossibility: what too of those photographic images made in the darkroom that involve contact printing? What about the cyanotypes and non-silver processes, not to mention the photogram, vortigraph, luminogram, scannergram, and radiograph? My *"flowgraphs"* (darkroom abstractions from the 1990s), and my movies such as *Angular Momentum* (recorded in a dark room with a digital DSLR camera), as well as my *Instaglitch* series all belong to this tradition of abstract photography. Avoiding those problems by declaring them "new" media enables the maintenance of "photography" as a discrete *pure* entity, unaffected by their existence.[83] And what of all those images made by physical objects that become the literal, physical template for the picture that results—an immediate correspondence, like a footprint left on the beach—are these photographs to be denied, even though that is clearly what they are and how they are identified?[84] To embrace the full range of photographic process is to lose the sense of restriction that fixes the idea of photography as a "natural" image of reality. Questions of abstraction become plausible and inevitable.

Marginalia are a way to consider these questions about the nature of the photograph. Familiar, typical images actually tell us little; it is only at the edges where things happen. There is little to say about what photographs *are* from the typical snapshots produced easily and then immediately forgotten, saved in a shoebox somewhere, simply because there is no doubt about their status as photographs. Much can be said about memory, time passed and recalled, their ability to return a past moment to immediacy, but all these things depend on their *realism*, that the photograph appears to be an inscription of the natural world apparent to our senses, one whose recalling into immediacy is a mere matter of what the image shows—yet what is at stake with abstract photography is what the image *is*.

But this question about *being* is the one photographers generally ignore, concerned with the mechanics of the machine they operate, considering how to create their images, found like the detritus of reality and recorded for later presentation. Theorizing the perfect moment for this imaging brings their search for 'the real' into focus as an attentive *flâneurism* that imposes distance between viewer and the world in an attempt to stitch the two ever more tightly together. Abstraction, real

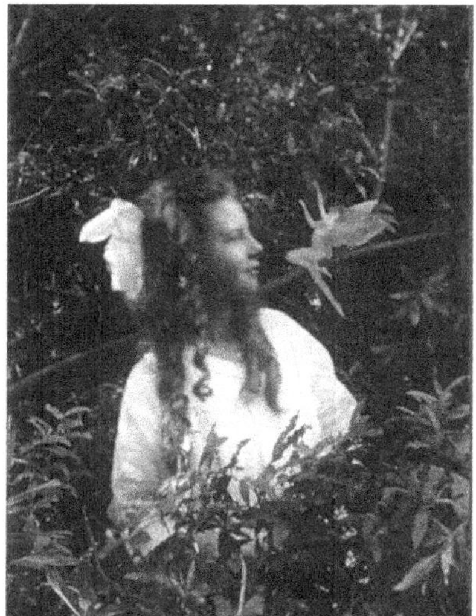
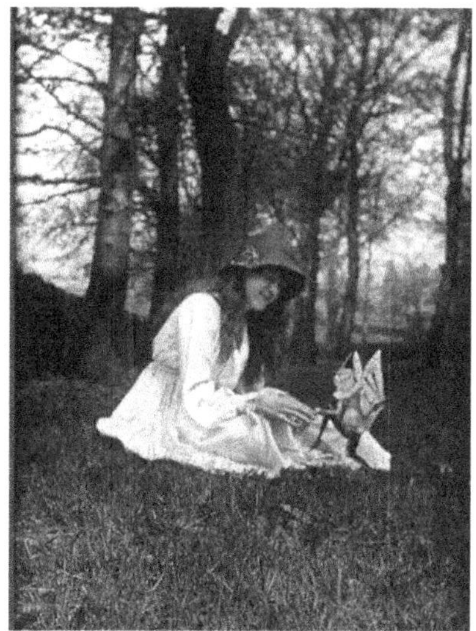

Figure 5.2: Elsie Wright and Frances Griffiths, photographs from their staged documentation of the *Cottingley Fairies,* 1917.

abstraction, divorced from this recording of actuality and its derivative assumptions about naturalism and a material order of sight, reveals the claim to capture reality as a lie.

Abstraction is forbidden, not because it is impossible, but because it resulted from photography forcing painting to turn inwards, to emphasize subjective experience over the objective documenting of a reality whose depiction the photograph automated.[85] For photography to turn to abstraction is the original violation, a refusal of its role as reporter of reality. The photograph has served to demarcate the actual against the fantasies and subjectivities of metaphysical, esoteric knowledge. This role is the secret truth of the "spirit photograph" whose translucent figures are nothing more than a double exposure or other darkroom trickery, facilitated and made simple by the digital darkroom and computer. It is the certainty that "Nessie" is a three-inch tall plastic toy bobbing in the water. The *Cottingley Fairies* are paper dolls [Figure 5.2]. These fakes are not abstraction, but the epistolary of *realism*: their unmasking, in being false, asserts and reveals a deeper truth, claiming the photograph does not actually lie, it is only the humans who do not see clearly enough. The issue of their depiction is not the fabrication of reality. Their discovery as fakes allows and affirms a restoration of 'the real' through the negation of their "proof"—what these images show or don't show is just a mundane product of human failings, not the machine's operation, a *mis*function that only fools credulous viewers. Once unmasked, the audience can congratulate themselves on their certainty about the reality shown (but hidden).[86]

Abstract photography undoes any certainty about reality; there is nothing to return to, nothing to unmask. The abstract photograph is itself, not a depiction resembling something in the world. Those contents its audience might think they recognize become the same uncertain visualization that metamorphic images and optical illusions pose: while there is clearly an image, what it shows is open to discussion, moving within boundaries fixed in such a way that the images seen are not the image shown. Those recognitions of the depicted reality in a photograph are certain and immobile, but once the ambivalence of the abstract is allowed inside the edifice of photography, that technological view of the world must necessarily expand—but it is an expansion that undoes its authoritative claims on reality. To recognize a photograph, any photograph, as composed from a network of grains or pixels whose joining together creates the realistic image its audience sees is to return that image to the realm of abstraction in a denial of the machine's autonomy as depictor. The machine that creates the image enters a powerful decline with the expansion of address created by embracing the abstract as the focus, and the concept of photography shifts from the autonomous device to the mind that sees and understands.

These difficulties of the still photograph are expanded upon by the motion picture, *realism* elevated to an axiomatic status via the dominant ideologies of cinema—theories which cannot distinguish between fiction and documentary film,[87] and seek to support their restrictive understanding of photography simply

---

Figure 5.3: untitled "flowgraph"
copyright © 1991 Michael Betancourt
courtesy Artists Rights Society (ARS)

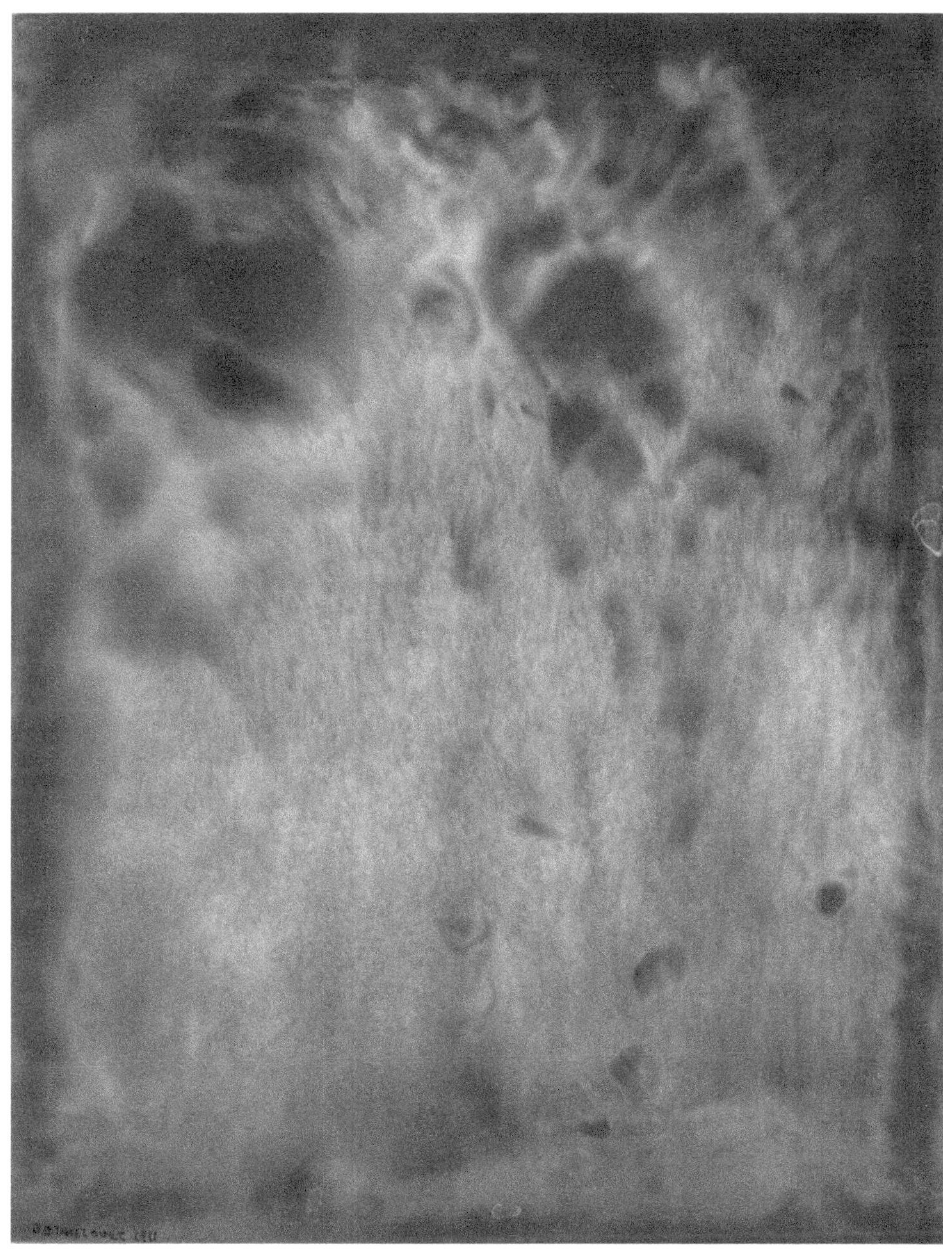

by ignoring all those works that challenge their beliefs.[88] Digital cinema, commencing in the 1990s, and accelerating throughout the first two decades of the twenty-first century brings all the problems posed by abstraction into the foreground as the concerns with photography metastize into a terminal crisis.[89] The digital glitch further unmasks the tenuous relationship of reality to photograph through its obvious ease of manipulation and fluid transformation between cartoonish imagery and highly detailed *realism*. The difference between computer graphics and digital photography is an issue of nomenclature, rather than technology: the image itself is the same whatever name it has. A capacity for abstraction has always been immanent in digital technology, whose basis in the regular grid of illuminated squares on-screen has a close affinity to the highly reductive geometries of art posed in painting by De Stijl, Suprematism, and Constructivism.[90]

My engagement with abstract photography comes as a cyclical return to foundations: my earliest abstract photographs, the series of "*flowgraphs*" [Figures 5.3 and 5.4], are purely products of the darkroom made without the intervention of traditional negatives, optics, or objects. They are produced following this protocol for B&W photography:

> [**1**] Mix developer with a few grains of powdered laundry detergent in a shallow black pan to produce layers of differing density.
>
> [**2**] Take a sheet of photopaper and expose it to light in the normal fashion, but without printing an image.
>
> [**3**] Place this sheet in the pan, and solarize it. The amount of agitation in the solution during the solarization controls what kind of image results.
>
> [**4**] Wash the paper and finish developing it normally.

The resulting print is actually a negative image of the liquid flows which produced it, placing that image in the same category as

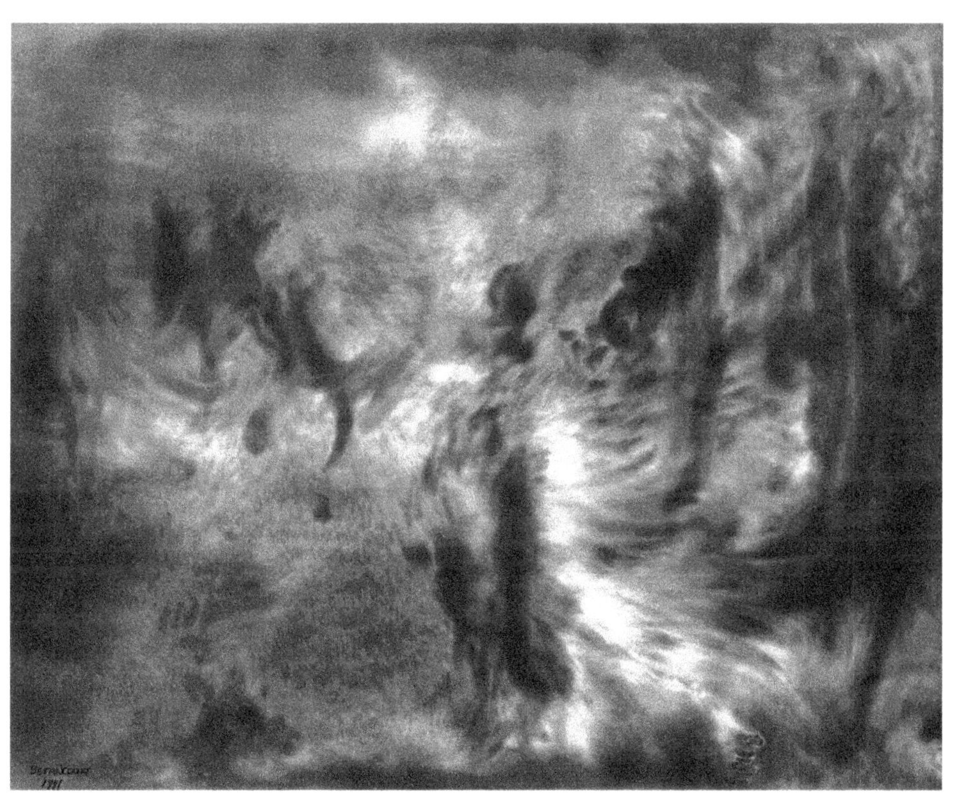

Figure 5.4: untitled “flowgraph”
copyright © 1991 Michael Betancourt
courtesy Artists Rights Society (ARS)

other photographic negatives. This process developed uniquely thorough experiment and my own darkroom work; however, the resulting images recall abstract darkroom compositions produced by Vance Bor, Raul Ubac, and Roger Parry fifty years earlier, in the 1920s–1940s.[91] My early darkroom concerns with non-traditional imaging processes return with the development in the 2010s of high sensitivity digital cameras that respond to light fluctuations and dynamics that were formerly impossible to image with either analogue video or photochemical motion picture films—and which I employed to make movies such as *Angular Momentum* (2019) [Figure 5.5]. This technology enabled a direct return to iconography linked to the motion of light, but which was sublimated into graphic animation and digital processing (such as the *Instaglitch* series).

The question of abstract photography is thus the same problem posed by the digital; it brings entire realms of artificial and unreal images generated and created through machines into the consideration of what defines the photograph, an expansion whose operative impact is definitive. Abstract photography demonstrates the belief in an inherent and inescapable *realism* is a fallacy, nothing more than an artifice, a carefully produced appearance made through a precisely controlled mechanism. All those values which we associate with the photograph—documentation, reality, certainty—are simply functions of its autonomous operation and the historical difficulties with creating abstract images using this machine designed for *realism*. To apprehend the abstract photograph then is to have cultural uses laid bare in a return to 'zero.' It is ideology that makes photography into the 'real,' not the ontology of the photograph. And this is the real danger of abstraction, the suggestion that there is more to see than meets the eyes, that vision is limited and often mistaken, needing correctives no optician can prescribe. The regulation of sight is the definition of reality; the acceptance or invalidation of abstraction serves to make certain orderings acceptable and others forbidden. For the photograph, abstraction is the first, and always the most fundamentally *unheimlich* glitch.

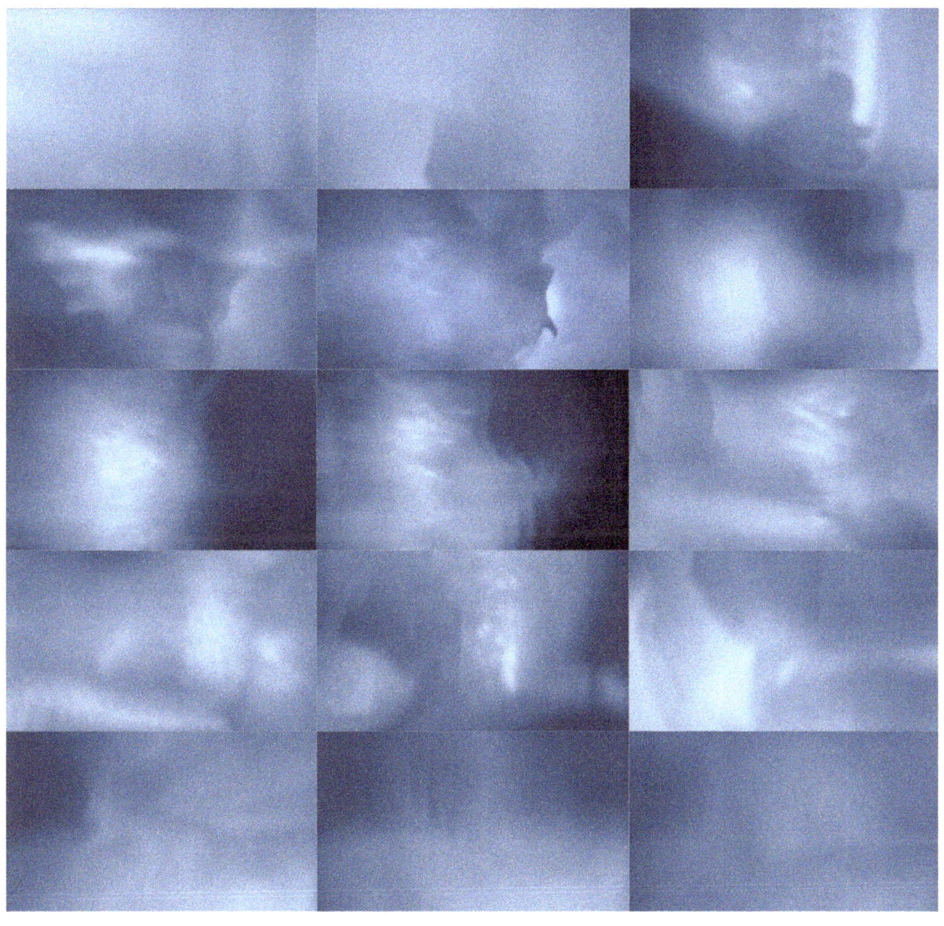

Figure 5.5: Stills from *Angular Momentum* (2019)
copyright © 2019 Michael Betancourt
courtesy Artists Rights Society (ARS)

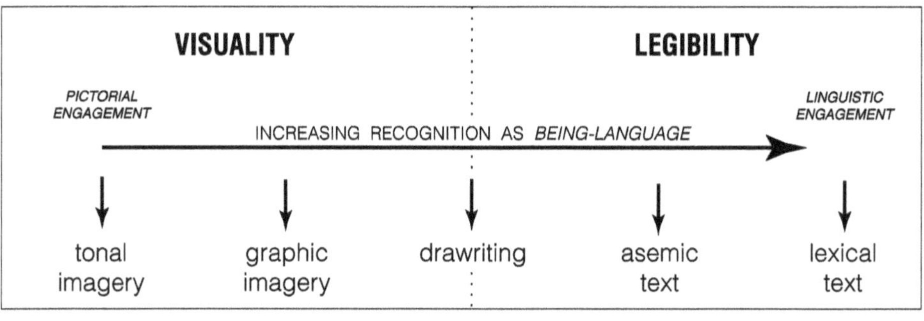

Figure 6.1: The categorical range of 'lexical function' identifies the articulation of both visual forms, the recognitions of language, and the interpretive act of reading—as well as the intermedial forms that create the overlaps between them.

6
LEXICAL GLITCHES

Typoetry is a portmanteau word made from the combination of "typography" and "poetry," but also evokes the abbreviation for errors in typesetting, the "typo," that renders text alexical (asemic). The perceptual ambivalence and ambiguity it produces for its would-be readers converges on digital glitches, but exists purely in the recognitions of language. It identifies a variety of visual poetry made by manipulating and fragmenting typography so that its *transparent* identity comes into question: these exploratory and experimental works approach writing via encounters with the printed page.[92] Typoetry arises from residues of language—neither a challenge to the communicative language, nor a refusal of the transparency of reading[93]—it adheres to Ferdinand de Saussure's theorization of those semiotics that defy the allocations of fixed or final meaning:

> Language does not present itself to us as a set of signs already delimited, requiring us merely to study their meanings and organization. It is an indistinct mass, in which attention and habit alone enable us to distinguish particular elements. The unit has no special phonic character, and the only definition it can be given is the following: a segment of sound which is, as distinct from what preceded and follows in the spoken sequence, the signal of a certain concept.[94]

Consideration of typoetry is instructive for understanding the critical potentials of visual media—even if the works themselves are not explicitly works of critical art, they provide a clear demonstration of the interpretive process, and thus provide an aesthetic space in which problems of interpretation can have 'free play.' However, Typoems should be regarded as neither a demonstration of theory, nor are they readily illuminated by considering their form in terms of "encoded" intentions as with everyday languages.[95] A critically discursive approach to signification distracts from the particulars of their articulation.[96] What you see is what you see: the active decision to engage perception *as-if* it was a vehicle of symbolic meaning (i.e. intentionally encoded) arises from the audience imposing signification but not theorizing its arrangement.[97] The legibility of cultural signifiers[98] conceives those terms in the range [Figure 6.1] between visual works and lexical forms as a lacuna, a nebulous zone of implied order, their "enunciative intrusion" illuminating the role of "model texts" for lexia.[99]

Writing originates in perception, but creates meaning that is circumstantially sensitive, dependent on multiple recognitions that reframe and reinterpret perception in predictable ways that Eco described as "recognition." It depends on enculturation, that process of *transparency* productive of the linguistic fluency necessary to fill-in the missing parts of words and letterforms:

> Recognition occurs when a given object or event, produced by nature or human action (intentionally or unintentionally), and existing in a world of facts as a fact among facts, comes to be viewed by an addressee as the expression of a given content, either through a pre-existing and coded correlation or through the positing of a possible correlation by its addressee.[100]

Eco's insight that interpretation depends on an *as-if* engagement converges on psychological experiments with language identification and recognition: as in Haslerud and Clark's experiments with letter and word recognition when forms are obscured or missing,[101] or in work by Solomon and Postman where *familiarity* was a predictor for how easily a word or letter would be identified.[102] These aspects of perceptual psychology[103] also become apparent in the recognitions of

---

Figure 6.2: *Typoem 2021-07* copyright © 2021 Michael Betancourt courtesy Artists Rights Society (ARS)

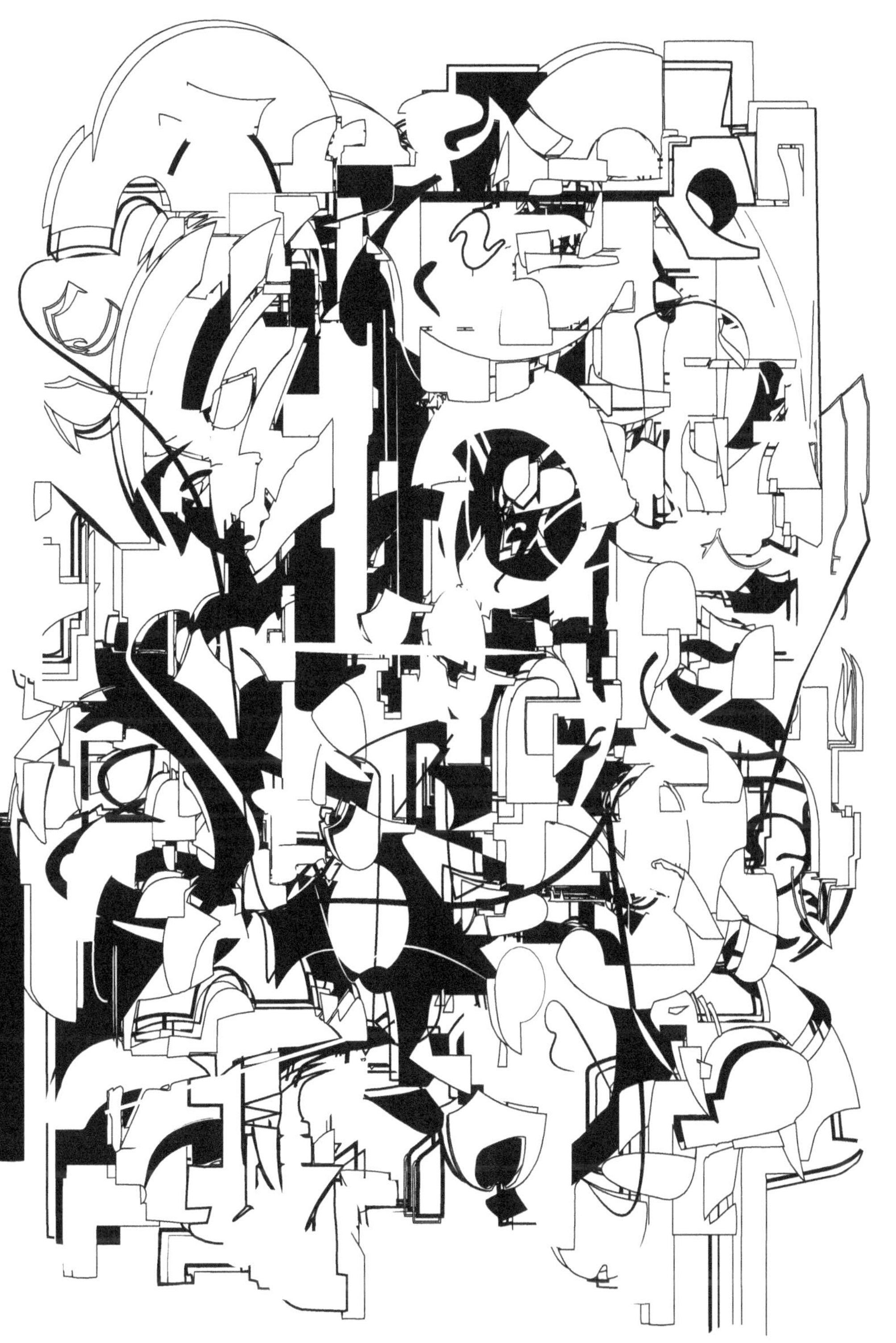

language-without-lexicality that are typical of all asemic works; enculturation is an inherent constraint for semiosis because it is always limited by the reader's proximate awareness.[104] The integration of signs (even asemic ones) is derived from how perception requires knowledge gained from past experience to become coherent.[105]

Although the centrality of past experience and established knowledge is apparent in those interpretations that modify the experiential encounter (a top-down constraint on perception), Eco's concern is with the communication of a specific meaning, not how perceptions delimit identification. His semiotics does not directly address what concerns typoetry: the capacity of visual-but-alexical dimensions of written words to inflect, deflect, and modify the meaning of lexical text precisely matches the impacts that glitches have on the identification and recognition of visual imagery.

These dynamics demonstrate that the theoretical and critical interest of *typoetry* is more than merely as a meditation on what graphic design theorizes as "invisible typography."[106] The assertion of communication as the *only* valence of/for text is an expression of Modernist concerns with purity and medium-specificity. Typoety challenges this basis in the same way that all glitches efface comfortable category boundaries and distinctions—it is what unifies them in praxis, if not in articulated significance. This foundational constraint (the *legibility* of the typography) appears historically in the hesitancy to violate the integrity of letterforms, even when their lexicality is being held in suspension, as the asemic poet Nico Vassilakis explains:

> I see no reason to destroy word, I simply want to undo word so the letters become revealed. Letters gather in a pre word formation, free to move about and explore before they are forced to line up and take their place in a word sequence. I see the letters as ingredients without which words would not exist.[107]

This poet's concern with language makes the same foundational concern with legibility apparent that guides the typical uses of typography: as a vehicle for communication. The unity and stability of either letterforms, words, or the statements composed from them cannot be assumed in typoetry—the familiarity and stability of letterforms is precisely what is suspended by typoems specifically (as lexicality is by asemic poetry generally). Historical works approaching this same breakdown and fragmentation of letterforms were constrained by the intransigent nature of type itself: a physical material arranged and situated on the page, it could only come into being via printing. The typoetry created by Hansjörg Mayer (who invented this type of visual poetry) makes these technical constraints apparent.[108] Overlaps, repetitions, and layering obscure and complicate physical letterforms but do not violate their integral identification. The '*identify*' of his letter-elements is never in question, a reflection of the constraints and demands made by his medium, physical typography and traditional printing.

However, with the shift from physical typography to the electronic vectorized type of digital design, the capacity to create typoetry that directly engages letterforms and their recognitions as a plastic material became possible: the technical potential of design software such as *Adobe Illustrator* to fluidly convert positive and negative spaces of digital fonts into physical materials for manipulation are demonstrated by the typoem. The foundation of each composition is resolutely and unquestionably focused on violating the familiar, Modernist conception of lettering, kerning, layering, and hierarchy[109] as invisible materials. These designs modulate the fundamental semantic identification of 'language' to draw attention to the semic/asemic distinction. Shifts in recognition are cued by/via the physical materials employed in constructing each composition; typoetry reveals what Michel Foucault identified as the foundations of semiosis and language in *The Archaeology of Knowledge*:

> The statement is neither a syntagma, nor a rule of construction, nor a canonic form of succession and permutation; it is that which enables such groups of signs to exist, and enables these rules or forms to become

> manifest. But although it enables them to exist, it does so in a special way—a way that must not be confused with the existence of signs as elements of a language (*langue*), or with the material existence of those marks that occupy a fragment of space or last for a variable length of time.[110]

These general observations were expanded in his discussion of the relationship between language and image in Rene Magritte's eponymous painting in the book *This is not a Pipe:*

> For the text to shape itself, for all its juxtaposed signs to form a dove, a flower, a rainstorm, the gaze must refrain from any possible reading. Letters must remain points, sentences lines, paragraphs surfaces or masses—wings, stalks, or petals. The text must say nothing to this gazing subject who is a viewer, not a reader. As soon as they begin to read, in fact, shape dissipates.[111]

Refusals of visuality give shape to the materials themselves: built from fragmented letterforms and their negative spaces, they combine accumulated fluency, extratextual experience, and intertextual knowledge with perception. Drawing conclusions from what are experiential works invites intentional fallacies and teleological justifications: while they originate with typography and digital fonts, what actually appears is what emerges when those vectorized instructions are a plastically transformable field[112] unmoored from their regimented identity as letterforms. Typoetry depends on the fluid transformability of digital software.[113] The example in Figure 6.2 is derived from *Helvetica,* an iconic typeface of the mid-twentieth century that is purified of all excesses to leave only the elements necessary for their (problematized) lexicality.

The explicit goal of Modernist graphic design, proposed at its inception by Bauhaus educator Jan Tschichold's *The New Typography* (1926) argued that the focus of typographic

---

Figure 6.3: *Typoem 2021-75* copyright © 2021 Michael Betancourt courtesy Artists Rights Society (ARS)

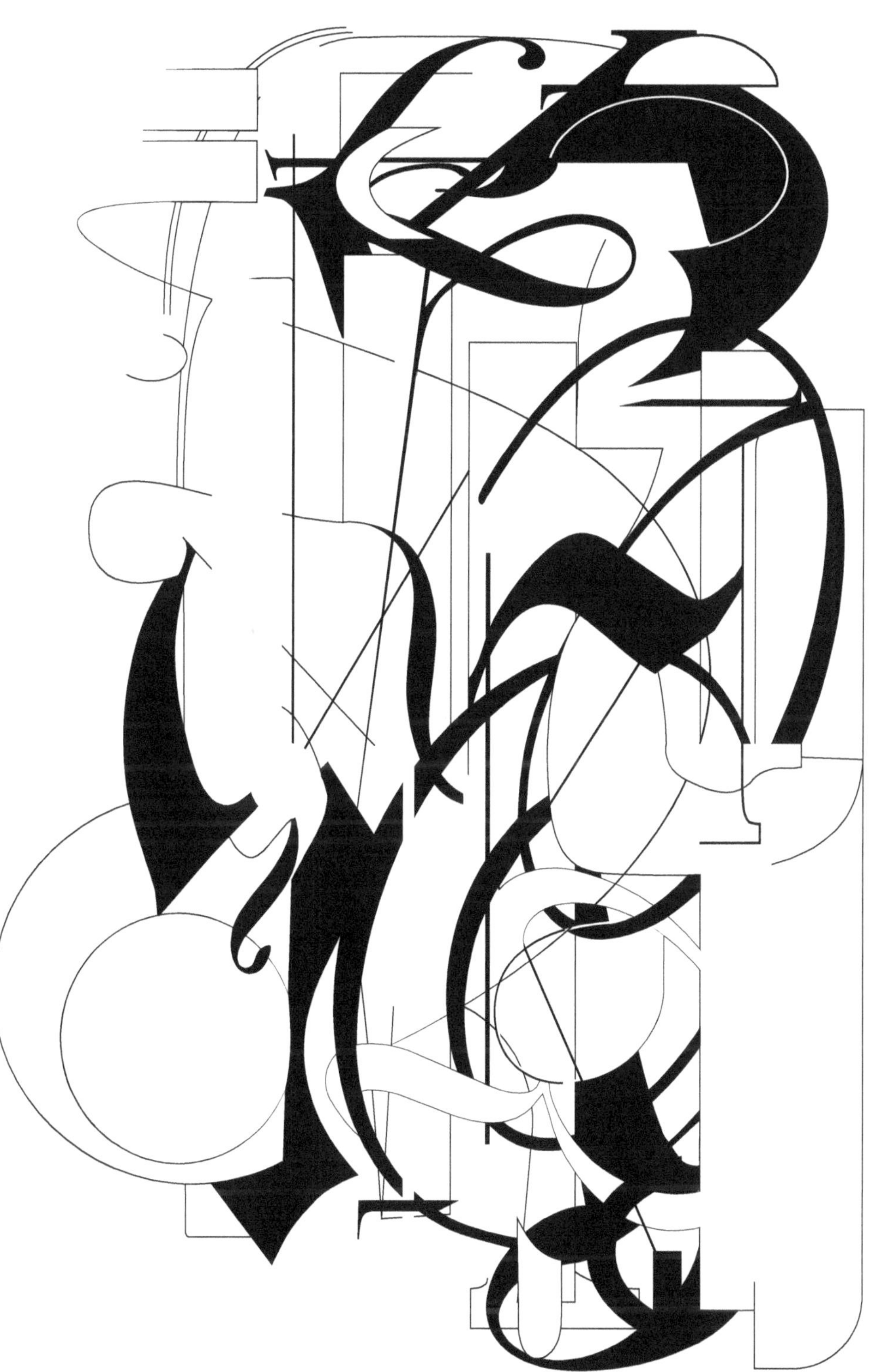

expressiveness is limited to what the words mean.[114] His proposal was echoed after World War II by design theorist Beatrice Warde, who argued that the function of design is to be maximally *legible*. Her metaphoric "transparency" means typography is "invisible" to the reader, as she explains in her essay "The Crystal Goblet, or Printing Should be Invisible":

> The most important thing about printing is that it conveys thought, ideas, images, from one mind to other minds. This statement is what you might call the front door of the science of typography. Within lie hundreds of rooms, but unless you start by assuming that printing is meant to convey specific and coherent ideas, it is very easy to find yourself in the wrong house altogether.[115]

This approach, embraced by Modernist type designers such as Aicher, Frutiger, Goudy, or Ruder, assumes there is only a singular, universal significance for text—established by the intentions of the author/designer, and the goal of typography is to enable the *transparent mode* that renders this hypothetical intent clearly and without modification. "Invisibility" ignores the encultured and learned aspects of lexical engagement; it is the demand for text to communicate, as well as the rejection of glitches as "noise." This fundamentally passive concern with "content" necessarily limits how the reader is "allowed" to comprehend and engage the work: it only 'authorizes' certain understandings, creating the apparent stability of the knowledge it communicates.[116] Such a *modus operandi* contradicts what semiotician Roman Jakobson has described as the 'poetic function' of language that is derived from all the non-linguistic dimensions of articulation in lexical *parole*, (such as expressions of emotion), that the *transparency* sought by these designers necessarily denies and minimizes. The materiality of the design/presentation articulates meaning distinctly and in contradistinction to that of the legible content of the letters/words—and these aspects are the focus of typoetry: the expressiveness of the letters and their capacity to evoke meaning apart from their semic dimensions.

The arrangement and structure of typoetry (derived from the standardized, uniform marks of type) develops in parallel to the drawn letterforms of asemic handwriting, adapting the effacement of signification to typography while retaining the cues that identify these compositions as being-language, even if their informational dimensions as-communication are in suspension. Exploiting the expressive potentials of letterforms is hardly new, but in these Janus-like visual gestalts the lexical recognition becomes, a meditation on the perfect moment where perceptions become meaningful and the semiotic chain begins its inexorable progress towards what semiotician Hartmut Stöckl ascribed to the graphic dimensions of language:

> Typefaces may point to the nature of the document, carry emotional values, or indicate the writer's intended audience, and aspects of the layout may serve to reinforce the thematic structure of a given text and facilitate access to its information. Finally, on yet another level of typographic meaning making, the graphic signs of writing can assume pictorial qualities. Thus, letters may form visual shapes which stand for objects from reality, signal states-of-affairs or actions, and illustrate emotions. Materials and techniques of graphic sign making, too, may be made salient in text design and can thus convey something about situation, genre and stylistic intent of a communicative occurrence—this is also a pictorial kind of communication. It is this threefold semiotic nature of typography that provides its communicative flexibility.[117]

Legibility is assumed in visual poetry: if not as coherent words, then as letters remaining familiar, coherent, recognizable.[118] The "pictorial qualities" he describes are readily apparent in the non-lexical visualities shown by the various traditions of calligraphy as well as in visual poetry (a term that covers a wide range of practices that includes calligrams, concrete poems, and asemic handwriting), where they emerge uniformly from artistic exploits of the graphic foundation of writing as markings.[119] This proposition is apparent in how the spaces around or between forms echoes a "protentional expectation"[120] that externalizes the knowledge that arises from and overlaps with these *graphic expressions* that are neither familiar letter shapes, nor not-lettering.[121] They reward contemplation and engagement with the faces of typographic characters in the same ways that lexical poetry does, as Gestalt psychologist Rudolph Arnheim noted:

> The structure of the whole, certainly of dominant importance, is influenced by the parts, which in turn depend on the whole as to their shapes and interrelations. Neither the whole nor the parts are primary constants, primordial executives of influence. Rather, all components from the whole to the smallest detail exert their modifying effect, while they are being modified.[122]

The premise that visual poetry needs to be and reward only immediate contemplations stifles the potentials for greater complexity. Typoetry offers a counteractive to negation: they neither have, nor are designed to have the instant recognition followed by immediate forgetting typical of logos and brand marks as in visual poetry by Derek Beaulieu, Richard Kostelanz, Geoff Huth, Donato Mancini, or Christian Bok. These typoems are meditations on a "natural technical evolution"—as in the transformative visuals based on letterforms by Norman Ives, Scott Helmes, or Rosaire Appel. They are not monoidal constellations offering a fantasy that there is only one meaning; instead their interpretations proceed in ways that draw attention to the *as-if* of the reader's desires that find letterforms and familiarity among the graphic expressions of each composition.

These distinctions are not criticisms of earlier works. Different concerns and interests necessarily create radically different works, and the realm of visual and asemic poetry is no different in that regard that any other. This exploration/

Figure 6.4: *Typoem 2021-87* copyright © 2021 Michael Betancourt courtesy Artists Rights Society (ARS)

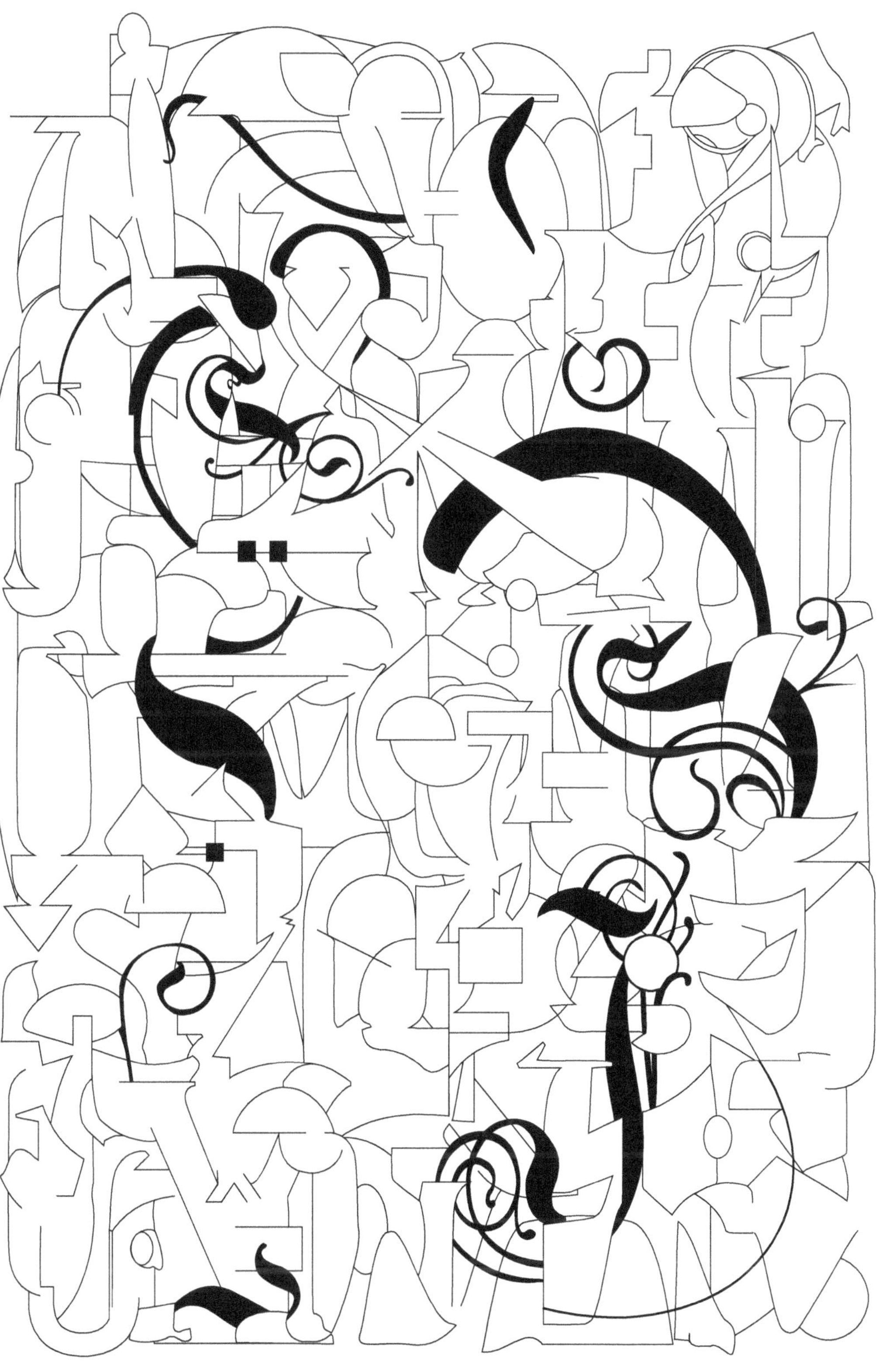

development of typoetry specifically depends on the capacities of digital technology to "open up" the letterforms to manipulation and modification. Typoetry makes the immediate category assignment, *written language,* apparent in the series of recognitions that become literally visible: this focus defines the typoem as a variety of asemic poetry, one that addresses foundational recognitions constitutive of typography and design in general.

Typoetry provides an experiential overlap between my purely visual interests, semiotic concerns, and the theoretical questions arising from marginalia such as glitches. It serves as an exploratory field where language and visual art intersect, but because Typoems are digitally-mediated productions, their creation also addresses novel and historically undeveloped potentials of typography and design: the asemic realm where the identification of the work as-language is always the primary recognition, an encounter that typoetry problematizes, allowing its consideration independently from semantics and meaning.

NOTES

Chapter 1

1 Cage, J. *Silence* (Middleton: Wesleyan University Press, 2011) p. 68.

2 Danto, A. *Beyond the Brillo Box* (Berkeley: University of California Press, 1990) p. 15.

3 Greenberg, C. "Modernist Painting" *The Collected Essays and Criticism: Vol. 4*, (Chicago: University of Chicago Press, 1955).

4 Krauss, R. "Sculpture in the Expanded Field" *The Anti-Aesthetic* ed. Hal Foster (Seattle: Bay Press, 1983) pp. 31-42.

5 Aira, C. *On Contemporary Art* trans. Katherine Silver (New York: David Zwirner Books, 2018) p. 26.

6 Schumpeter, J. *Capitalism, Socialism, and Democracy* (New York: Harper Perennial, 2008) p. 83.

7 Warhol, A. *The Philosophy of Andy Warhol* (New York; Harvest, 1976) p. 92.

8 Smith, T. "Contemporary Art and Contemporaneity" in *Critical Inquiry,* Vol. 32, No. 4 (Summer 2006).

9 Johnson, C. B. *Modernity Without a Project* (Brooklyn: Punctum Books, 2014).

10 Smith, Terry. "Contemporary Art and Contemporaneity" in *Critical Inquiry,* Vol. 32, No. 4 (Summer 2006), p. 688.

11 Smith, P. *Andy Warhol's Art and Films* (Ann Arbor: UMI Research Press, 1986).

12 Noll, A. M. "Computers and the Visual Arts" reprinted from *Design and Planning* no. 2, nd., np.

13 Schiller, D. *Digital Capitalism: Networking the Global Market System* (New Haven: The MIT Press, 1999).

14 Bourriaud, N. *Relational Aesthetics* trans. Simon Pleasance and Fronza Woods, (Dijon-Quetigny: Les Presses du Reel, 2004) pp. 48.

Chapter 2

15 Betancourt, M. "The 'Material Function' in Cinema: Resolving the Paradox of the Glitch" *Semiotica: Journal of the International Association for Semiotic Studies*, no. 236-237, 2020, pp. 251-273. DOI: https://doi.org/10.1515/sem-2019-0006

16 Brown, S. "Introduction" Synthesis: Processing and Collaboration (San Diego: The Gallery@Calit2, 2011).

17 Menkman, R. *Network Notebooks 4: The Glitch Moment(um)* (Amsterdam: Institute of Network Cultures, 2011) p. 35.

18 Brecht, B. "Alienation Effects in Chinese Acting" *Brecht on Theater: The Development of an Aesthetic* ed. and trans. J. Willet (New York: Hill and Wang, 1992) p. 92.

19 Jentsch, E. "*On the Psychology of the Uncanny* (1906)" trans. Roy Sellars, *Angelaki* 2.1 (1995) pp. 7-16.

20 Irei, N. "'Abolishing Aesthetics': *Gestus* in Brecht's *Arturo Ui*" *Rocky Mountain Review,* vol. 70, no. 2 (Fall 2016) p. 150.

21 Brecht, B. "The Popular and the Realistic" *Brecht on Theater: The Development of an Aesthetic* ed. and trans. J. Willet (New York: Hill and Wang, 1992) p. 108-109.

22 Betancourt, M. "Critical Glitches and Glitch Art" *Harmonia: Glitch, Movies and Visual Music* (Rockport: Wildside Press, 2018) pp. 149-172.

23 Weyler, K. "Seriality and Susanna Rowson's *Sincerity*" *Legacy: A Journal of American Women Writers* vol. 34, no. 1 (2017) p. 169.

24 Eco, U. *The Limits of Interpretation* (Bloomington: Indiana University Press, 1990) p. 92.

25 Freud, S. "*The Uncanny* (1919)" trans. Alix Strachey, accessed online, February 2, 2018 http://web.mit.edu/allanmc/www/freud1.pdf

26 Robinson. D. *Estrangement and the Somatics of Literature* (Baltimore: Johns Hopkins University Press, 2008) p. 199.

27 Martens, G. and Biebuyck, B. "Channeling figurativity through narrative: The Paranarrative in Fiction and Non-Fiction" *Literature and Language*, vol. 22, no. 3, pp. 249-262.

28 Eco, U. *The Limits of Interpretation* (Bloomington: Indiana University Press, 1990) p. 91.

29 Robinson. D. *Estrangement and the Somatics of Literature* (Baltimore: Johns Hopkins University Press, 2008) pp. 198-200.

30 Robinson, D. "The Spatiotemporal Dialectic of Estrangement" *TDR* vol. 51, no. 4 (Winter, 2007) pp. 123-124.

Chapter 3

31 Lotringer, S. and Virilio, P. *The Accident of Art* (New York: Semiotext(e), 2005) p. 74.

32 O'Doherty, B. *Inside the White Cube: The Ideology of the Gallery Space, Expanded Edition* (Berkeley: University of California Press, 1986).

33 Betancourt, M. *The Critique of Digital Capitalism* (Brooklyn: Punctum Books, 2016) pp. 56-60.

34 Wees, W.C. *Light Moving in Time: Studies in the Visual Aesthetics of Avant-Garde Film,* (Berkeley: University of California Press, 1992) pp. 137-146.

35 Tarasti, E. *Theory of Musical Semiotics* (Bloomington: Indiana University Press, 1994) pp. 73-76.

36 Popper, F. *Art of the Electronic Age* (New York: Abrams, 1993) pp. 179-181.

37 Betancourt, M. *Glitch Art in Theory and Practice: Critical Failures and Post-Digital Aesthetics* (New York: Routledge, 2017) pp. 49-72.

38 Willats, S. *Art and Social Function* (London: Ellipsis, 2000).

39 "The Glitch Issue: Making the Perfect Accident" *IDN: International Design Network Magazine* vol. 18, no. 3 (2011) np.

40 Cascone, K. "The Aesthetics of Failure: 'Post-Digital' Tendencies in Contemporary Computer Music" *Computer Music Journal* vol. 24, no. 4 (Winter, 2000) p. 17.

41 Brougher, K. *Visual Music: Art and Film Since 1900* (New York: Thames and Hudson, 2005).

42 Attali, J. *Noise: The Political Economy of Music* (Minneapolis: University of Minnesota Press, 1985) p. 6.

43 Cloninger, C. "GltchLnguistx: The Machine in the Ghosts / Static Trapped in the Mouths" *Glitch reader(ror)* ed. Nick Briz, Evan Meaney, Rosa Menkman, William Robertson, Jon Satrom, Jessica Westbrook (Unsorted Books: 2011) p. 33.

44 O'Doherty, B. *Inside the White Cube: The Ideology of the Gallery Space, Expanded Edition* (Berkeley: University of California Press, 1986).

45 Plato. "The Allegory of the Cave" *The Republic* trans. Thomas Sheehan sec. 514 a, 2 to 517 a, 7 https://web.stanford.edu/class/ihum40/cave.pdf accessed 20 April 2021.

46 Fer, B. *Abstract Art* (New Haven: Yale University Press, 1997) p. 149.

47 Brown, S. "Introduction" *Synthesis: Processing and Collaboration* (San Diego: The Gallery@Calit2, 2011) p. 5.

48 Larkin, B. "Degraded Images, Distorted Sounds: Nigerian Video and the Infrastructure of Piracy" *Public Culture* vol. 16, no. 2 (2004) p. 292.

49 Temkin, D. "Glitch && Human-Computer Interaction" *Non-Object Oriented Art* vol. 1, no. 1, (January, 2014).

50 Zinman, G. "Getting Messy: Chance and Glitch in Contemporary Video Art" *Abstract Video: The Moving Image in Contemporary Art* ed. Gabrielle Jennings (Oakland: University of California Press, 2015) p. 107.

51 Betancourt, M. "Critical Glitches and Glitch Art" *Hz,* no. 19 (July, 2014), np.

52 Adorno, T. *Aesthetic Theory* (Minneapolis: University of Minnesota Press, 1998) pp. 246-248.

53 Sonawane, S. and Pansambal, B. "Review of Artifacts In JPEG Compression And Reduction" International Journal of Advanced Research in Electronics and Communication Engineering (IJARECE) vol. 6, no. 3 (March, 2017) pp. 164-167.

54 Barker, T. "Aesthetics of the Error: Media Art, the Machine, the Unforseen, and the Errant" *Error: Glitch Noise and Jam in New Media Cultures,* ed. Mark Nunes (New York: Bloomsbury, 2011) pp. 46-48.

55 Melville, S. "Counting / As / Painting" *As painting: Division and Displacement* (Cambridge: MIT Press, 2001) pp. 1-27.

Chapter 4

56 Moradi, I. "Introduction" *Glitch: Designing Imperfection* ed. Iman Moradi, Ant Scott, Joe Gilmore and Christopher Murphy (New York: Mark Batty, 2009) pp. 8-9.

57 Ramey, K. *Experimental Filmmaking: Break the Machine* (Burlington: Focal Press, 2016) p. 365.

58 Russell, C. *Experimental Ethnography: The Work of Film in the Age of Video* (Durham: Duke University Press, 1999) pp. 238-239.

59 Cloninger, C. "GltchLnguistx: The Machine in the Ghosts / Static Trapped in the Mouths" in *Glitch reader(ror)* ed. Nick Briz, Evan Meaney, Rosa Menkman, William Robertson, Jon Satrom, Jessica Westbrook, (Unsorted Books: 2011), p. 35.

60 Youngblood, G. "A Medium Matures: Video and the Cinematic Enterprise" *Ars Electronica: Facing the Future* ed. Timothy Druckrey (New Haven: The MIT Press, 1999) pp. 45-46.

61 Brown, S. "Introduction" *Synthesis: Processing and Collaboration* (San Diego: The Gallery@Calit2: 2011), p. 5.

62 Zinman, G. "Getting Messy: Chance and Glitch in Contemporary Video Art" *Abstract Video: The Moving Image in Contemporary Art* ed. Gabrielle Jennings (Oakland: University of California Press, 2015) p. 107.

63 Temkin, D. "Glitch && Human-Computer Interaction" *Non-Object Oriented Art*, vol. 1, no. 1, (January, 2014).

64 Fielding, R. *The Technique of Special Effects Cinematography* (Oxford: Focal Press, 1984) pp. 405-406.

65 Sherman, Tom. "Vernacular Video" *INC Reader #4: Video Vortex Reader—Responses to YouTube* ed. Geert Lovink and Sabine Niederer (Amsterdam: Institute of Network Cultures, 2008) p. 162.

66 Walley, J. " 'Not an Image of the Death of Film': Contemporary Expanded Cinema and Experimental Film" *Expanded Cinema: Art Performance Film* ed. David Curtis, A.L. Rees, Duncan White and Steven Ball (London: Tate, 2011) p. 244.

67 Navas, E. *Remix-Theory: The Aesthetics of Sampling* (New York: Springer, 2012) pp. 22-27.

68 Eco, U. "Interpreting Serials" *The Limits of Interpretation* (Bloomington: University of Indiana Press, 1994) pp. 88-89.

69 Turkina, O. *Soviet Space Dogs* trans. Inna Cannon and Lisa Wasserman (London: Fuel, 2014) p. 143.

70 Betancourt, M. *Glitch Art in Theory and Practice: Critical Failures and Post-Digital Aesthetics* (New York: Routledge, 2016) pp. 86-100.

71 Betancourt, M. "Postcinema, Motion Perception and Glitch Movies" *AM Journal of Art and Media Studies* no. 15 (2018). doi: 10.25038/am.v0i15.242

72 Lowood, H. "Video Capture: Machinima, Documentation, and the History of Virtual Worlds" *The Machinima Reader* (Cambridge: The MIT Press, 2011) pp. 3-6.

73 Betancourt, M. *Ideologies of the Real in Title Sequences, Motion Graphics and Cinema* (New York: Routledge, 2019) pp. 177-191.

74 Attali, J. *Noise: The Political Economy of Music* (Minneapolis: University of Minnesota Press, 1985) p. 6.

Chapter 5

75 Phillips, C. *Photography in the Modern Era: European Documents and Critical Writing, 1913-1940* (New York: Aperture, 1989), p. 110.

76 Sontag, S. *On Photography* (New York: Anchor Books, 1977), p. 5.

77 Wall, J. "Marks of Indifference: Aspects of Photography in, or as, Conceptual Art" *Veronica's Revenge* ed. Elizabeth Janus, (New York: Scalo, 1998) p. 83.

78 Solomon-Godeau, A. "Photography After Art Photography" *Art after Modernism: Rethinking Representation* ed. Brian Wallis (New York: Godine, 1984), p. 82.

79 Solomon-Godeau, A. "Photography After Art Photography" *Art after Modernism: Rethinking Representation* ed. Brian Wallis (New York: Godine, 1984), pp. 76-82.

80 Visser, H. "What are Museums making of Photography?" *Veronica's Revenge* ed. Elizabeth Janus, (New York: Scalo, 1998) p. 227.

81 Roh, F. "Introduction" *Abstract Pictures on Film: The Technique of Making Light Graphics* (New York: Viking Press, 1964).

82 Barnes, M. *Cameraless Photography* (London: V&A Publishing, 2018).

83 Phillips, C. *Photography in the Modern Era: European Documents and Critical Writing, 1913-1940* (New York: Aperture, 1989), p. 211.

84 Scimè, G. "Forme come concetti" *Luigi Veronesi* (Milan: Gruppo Editoriate Fabbri, 1983) pp. 4-8.

85 Rexer, L. *The Edge of Vision* (New York: Aperture, 2009) pp. 14-15.

86 Baudrillard, J. *Simulations* (New York: Semiotexte, 1983) pp. 23-26.

87 Bazin, A. "The Myth of Total Cinema" *What is Cinema?* trans. Timothy Barnard (Montreal: Caboose, 2009) pp. 13-20.

88 Cavell, S. *The World Viewed: Reflections on the Ontology of Film (Enlarged Edition)* (Cambridge: Harvard University Press, 1979).

89 Hagener, M., Hediger V. and Strohmaier, A. *The State of Post-Cinema* (London: Palgrave, 2016) p. 3.

90 Noll, A. M. "Human or Machine: A subjective comparison of Piet Mondrian's *Composition With Lines* (1917) and a Computer-Generated Picture" *Psychological Record* vol. 16, no. 1 (1966) pp. 1-10.

91 Bajac, Q. and Chéroux, C. *La Subversion des Images* (Paris: Centre Pompidou, 2009).

Chapter 6

92 Bohn, W. *The Aesthetics of Visual Poetry: 1914-1928* (Chicago: University of Chicago Press, 1986) pp. 3-8.

93 Schwenger, P. *Asemic: The Art of Writing* (Minneapolis: University of Minnesota Press, 2019) pp. 34-60.

94 Saussure, F. *Course in General Linguistics* eds. Charles Bally and Albert Sechehaye, with the collaboration of Albert Rielinger, trans. Roy Harris (Chicago: Open Court, 1972) p. 102.

95 Schellong, M. "Moving Signs: Playing with Legibility and Aesthetic Experience" *Typemotion* ed. Bernd Scheffer, Christine Stenzer, Peter Weibel and Soenke Zehle (Karlsruhe: Hatje Cantz/ZKM, 2015) pp. 55-57.

96 Drucker, J. "What is a Word's Body?" *What is? Nine Epistemological Essays* (Victoria: Cuneform Press, 20130) p. 38.

97 Wainer, H. "Preface to the 2010 edition of the English Translation" *Semiology of Graphics* trans. William J. Berg (Redlands: Esri Press, 2010) pp. xi-xii.

98 McLuhan, M. *The Gutenberg Galaxy: The Making of Typographic Man* (Toronto: University of Toronto Press, 1962).

99 Eco, U. *A Theory of Semiotics,* (Bloomington: Indiana University Press, 1979) pp. 137-138.

100 Eco, U. *A Theory of Semiotics* (Bloomington: Indiana University Press, 1979) p. 221.

101 Haslerud, George M., and Clark, R. Ernest. "On the Redintegrative Perception of Words," *The American Journal of Psychology*, vol. 70, no. 1 (1957) pp. 100–101 DOI: 10.2307/1419236

102 Solomon, R. L., and Postman, L. "Frequency of Usage as a Determinant of Recognition Threshold for Words," *Journal of Experimental Psychology* vol. 43, no. 3, (1952) pp. 195-201 DOI: 10.1037/h0054636

103 von Hornbostel, E. "The Unity of the Senses," *A Source Book of Gestalt Psychology* ed. Willis D. Ellis (Gouldsboro: Gestalt Journal Press, 1997) p. 214.

104 Harris, R. *Introduction to Integrational Linguistics* (Oxford: Pergamon 1998) p. 105.

105 Harris, R. *Integrating Reality* (London: New Generation Publishing, 2012).

106 Warde, B. *The Crystal Goblet, Sixteen Essays on Typography* (London: Sylvan Press, 1955) pp. 11-17.

107 Vassilakis, N. *Voir Dire* (Dusie, 2020) p. 80.

108 Mayer, H. *Typo* (Köln: Walter König, 2014).

109 Golden, W. *The Visual Craft of William Golden* (New York: George Braziller, 1962) p. 21.

110 Foucault, M. *The Archaeology of Knowledge* (New York: Pantheon, 1972), p. 88.

111 Foucault, M. *This is not a Pipe* (Berkeley: University of California Press, 1983) p. 24.

112 Berry, D. and Dieter, M. "Thinking Postdigital Aesthetics: Art, Computation, Design" *The State of Post-Cinema* Berry, D. and Dieter, M eds. (New York: Palgrave Macmillan, 2015) pp. 2-3.

113 Brownie, B. *Transforming Type: New Directions in Motion typography* (New York: Bloomsbury, 2015) p. 15.

114 Tschichold, J. *The New Typography* trans. Ruari McLean (Berkeley: University of California Press, 1998).

115 Warde B. *The Crystal Goblet: Sixteen Essays on Typography* (London: Sylvan Press, 1955) p. 13.

116 Foucault, M. *The Archaeology of Knowledge* (New York: Pantheon, 1972).

117 Stöckl, H. "Typography: body and dress of a text" *Visual Communication 4.2,* (June 2005) p. 78.

118 Huth, G. "Visual Poetry Today" *Poetry* vol. 193, no. 2. (November, 2008) p. 127.

119 Betancourt, M. *Typography and Motion Graphics: The 'Reading-Image'* (New York: Routledge, 2018) pp. 68-101.

120 Stiegler, B. *Technics and Time 3: Cinematic Time and the Question of Malaise* (Stanford: Stanford University Press, 2011) p. 19.

121 Stiegler, B. *Technics and Time 1: The Fault of Epimetheus* (Stanford: Stanford University Press, 1998) p. 77.

122 Arnheim, R. *To The Rescue of Art: Twenty-Six Essays* (Berkeley: University of California Press, 1992), p. 205.

www.ingramcontent.com/pod-product-compliance
Lightning Source LLC
Chambersburg PA
CBHW050009040726
47599CB00014B/1287

* 9 7 8 0 9 7 9 3 2 1 5 0 4 *